John Frederick Maurice

The Balance of Military Power in Europe

John Frederick Maurice

The Balance of Military Power in Europe

ISBN/EAN: 9783744725439

Printed in Europe, USA, Canada, Australia, Japan

Cover: Foto ©ninafisch / pixelio.de

More available books at **www.hansebooks.com**

THE
BALANCE OF MILITARY POWER IN EUROPE

AN EXAMINATION OF

THE WAR RESOURCES OF GREAT BRITAIN
AND THE CONTINENTAL STATES

BY

COLONEL MAURICE

ROYAL ARTILLERY

PROFESSOR OF MILITARY ART AND HISTORY AT THE
ROYAL STAFF COLLEGE

WILLIAM BLACKWOOD AND SONS
EDINBURGH AND LONDON
MDCCCLXXXVIII

CONTENTS.

	PAGE
INTRODUCTION,	vii
THE BALANCE OF MILITARY POWER IN EUROPE,	1
I. RUSSIA AND ENGLAND,	29
II. GERMANY, FRANCE, AND BELGIUM,	65
III. GERMANY, RUSSIA, AND AUSTRIA,	131
IV. ITALY, TURKEY, AND ENGLISH ALLIANCES,	191
INDEX,	241

b

INTRODUCTION.

THE circumstances which led to the writing of the articles forming the substance of this book were as follows. About four years ago I was asked to contribute to the "Citizen Series"—now being published by Messrs Macmillan & Co.—a volume on "National Defences." I objected at first, that as the national defences of England depend on the navy, it was rather a subject for a sailor than a soldier. On the whole, however, I was persuaded that though it was necessary for me to consult some able sailor, the whole statement might be more conveniently furnished by me. From that time the question has been continually before my mind; but the more I have thought of it, the more impossible it has seemed to me to deal satisfactorily with it until there was, in some shape or other, before the public a statement, to which I could appeal, as to the warlike condition of other Powers.

What is necessary for the defence of the English Empire depends on what attack is likely to be made upon it.

Furthermore, as it has happened to me to know intimately almost all those who for many years past have been practically considering the question, I was aware that for many reasons the time was hardly ripe for bringing the subject in a satisfactory shape before the public. The result has been that, greatly I fear to the disgust of my excellent friend and editor, Mr Craik, I have been continually postponing the publication of the volume. In the course of last year circumstances changed.

The advent of Mr Smith to the War Office, and of General Brackenbury to the head of the Intelligence Department, led to the serious and earnest taking up of practical work of a kind that many of us had been praying for for years, and had begun to think past praying for. Notably the defence of our coaling-stations—which my friend the late Colonel Home had throughout his active life, in season and out of season, pressed upon the attention of successive Governments and on the country—began to be seriously taken up as a matter of practical politics. The subject had been referred to a Royal Commission as long ago as May 1879, when Lord Beaconsfield's Government was in office. But there did not seem to be any prospect of the stations being properly garrisoned, as well as fortified and armed, till Mr Smith took office, and, both in his first tenure, his short period of opposition, and his return to office, pressed for the taking of practical steps to maintain at all times in our distant possessions such garrisons as would enable us to resist a *coup de main*. Moreover, fortunately information as to the steps being taken both in this respect and in others to make our defences practical, and not visionary merely, was laid in such shape before the public, that it was possible to quote it without divulging any information which was not designed for the public ear.

It had been my duty also, for the purposes of my current work, to study with especial care during two years, the present condition of the armed Powers of Europe, and their military frontiers. Naturally, for a duty of importance to the future staff-officers of our army, I had facilities for obtaining knowledge which were not easily accessible to others.

Just at the moment when I was beginning to feel myself competent to speak with some authority on the subject, the following circumstances occurred.

First, Lord Wolseley very kindly allowed me to study in proof the exhaustive essay, which has since been published in Mr Ward's Jubilee volume, on the Past and Present of the English Army. That essay led to the conclusion that it is necessary for some authoritative non-party tribunal to determine the purposes for which we maintain our army and navy, to consider how far our present forces fulfil the necessary conditions, and to decide what forces we do or do not require to maintain.

Almost at the same time Sir James Fitz-James Stephen's Commission, amongst many other most valuable suggestions, made the same point.

In the course of conversation with me, Lord Wolseley had expressed the view that in the present condition of affairs we have the strongest interest in joining those Powers who desire to preserve peace, and in resisting those who threaten disturbance.

All the circumstances of the time seem to make it so probable that war may suddenly break out in more than one quarter of Europe, that I thought it probable that many readers would be interested in having such guidance as a careful preliminary study of the facts might enable me to supply as to the probable conditions under which war would take place, either between France and Germany or between Russia and Austria, with Germany on the side of Austria. I thought, also, that I saw my way to that statement in relation to the European forces which seemed to me essential as a preliminary to any discussion of "our national defences"; and therefore, for the purposes of the proposed volume, I was glad to seize it. Just at this moment an acquaintance of Sir Charles Dilke's put into my hand a proof of his last article of the series on 'The Position of European Politics'—that on the "United Kingdom." He asked me to notice certain expressions which Sir Charles Dilke had used about a recent speech of Lord Wolseley's, and to comment on them for Sir Charles Dilke's information. I had not seen Lord Wolseley since he had delivered the speech referred to; but as I was convinced that Sir Charles Dilke had misunderstood him, I wrote a series of comments which may now be read in Sir Charles Dilke's volume. For, to my no small surprise, I shortly afterwards found that my comments had been embodied in Sir Charles Dilke's article, with the statement that they represented Lord Wolseley's own explanation of his speech. As they did nothing of the kind, and, from the nature of the case, could not do so, I strongly conveyed that fact to Sir Charles Dilke, through our common acquaintance, before the article was sent to press; nevertheless he retained the words as he had originally written them. Naturally I was not disposed for any further communications of that character. I had, however, been reading the 'Fortnightly' articles with considerable interest, and as they had touched on the very subject I was anxious, for quite other reasons, to bring before the world, this incident led to my writing to Mr Blackwood proposing to deal in his Magazine with the question as a whole. I never have been, and, unless it be so to be a supporter of the Union, I am not now, a party man. I preferred, nevertheless, to ask Mr Blackwood to take the papers rather than any one else; because, looking at the matter solely as a question of justice, it seemed to me that Sir Charles Dilke had been curiously ill qualified, and had in his article shown himself so, to address "those who desire to put aside personal and party prejudice." He had fastened in his attack upon a minor incident of the broad scheme of reform, which owed its practical possibility to Mr Smith. He had given to it a false interpretation. It seems to me that, if we are ever to get things put on a proper footing, it is the bounden duty of all those who do not care for party to rally to the support of the first statesman, whoever he may be, who will seriously take up practical business. If that is partisanship, I am a partisan. I am certain—and it is the opinion of all those who have had the whole of the facts before them—that Sir Charles Dilke's words on that subject did nothing but mischief. He has since tried to avoid the issue [1] by saying that it is an irrelevant question whether Mr Smith was a good man of business or not. Certainly it is. I never raised it. It is

[1] See the whole passage, 'Fortnightly Review,' January 1888, p. 5.

Introduction. xiii

not an irrelevant issue whether the effect of Sir Charles's articles is or is not to move a vote of no confidence in a particular statesman, precisely because he attempted to provide us with effective garrisons for our coaling-stations and harbours, and to enable our *corps d'armée* to act in the field. If to say that you will only believe these things when you see them,[1] as Sir Charles Dilke specifically did, be not to declare "no confidence," and if that be not the ordinary English mode of expressing a wish to displace a statesman, I do not understand what words mean.

I am anxious, however, to avoid making this Introduction or these articles into a mere controversy with Sir Charles Dilke. Considering the amount of attention which his articles had attracted, it was almost impossible to avoid noticing those points on which I agreed or differed from him. But my purpose has been to deal with questions only incidentally alluded to by Sir Charles Dilke.

In the article under the general heading of the "Balance of Power in Europe," my object has been to show historically, that in the cases in modern times in which we have had any interest in intervening on the Continent, we could have, in fact, intervened with decisive effect. I have, in order to show this, dealt with the cases of Denmark in 1864,

[1] 'Present Position of European Politics,' p. 316.

and of Constantinople in 1878. My complaints as to Sir Charles Dilke's statements on these subjects were, in fact, little better than pegs on which to hang certain historical statements, on which, for the purposes of my general contention, I am most anxious to insist. The appearance of Mr Kinglake's new volumes has enabled me to reinforce these statements by appealing to his account of the Kertch Expedition, and to his admirable comments on that incident, as well as to the legitimate deductions from what he has now proved to have been the true story of the siege of Sebastopol itself.

The deduction which it is my object to draw from these records of the past is that, to quote Mr Kinglake again, the places "where land and sea much intertwine" are those where the power of England can best be exerted. Further, that the power which we can there exert does not depend on our navy alone, but upon the marvellous force we possess in our unrivalled mercantile marine. That there is a quite peculiar and enormously potent military influence which may be exerted by a small army which can be landed at pleasure at unknown points by a nation which possesses the command of the sea. That, in order to make that force available, it is indispensable that it should be warlike—not merely military—in its composition: in other words, that it is useless to ship in this way mere regiments, batteries, and squadrons, but that the force must consist of perfect little armies, such as are formed by the *corps d'armée* of the Continent. That, from the nature of the conditions under which we must always enter upon war, it is more—not less—necessary for us than for Continental Powers to have the force with which we are to act ready for instant action, not on a parade or at an Aldershot review, but on a field of battle and throughout a campaign. That, nevertheless, our whole military power disappears unless our navy is so overwhelmingly powerful that it will be able to spare force for striking blows away from home, and will not be absorbed in mere defence of our shores and of our vast commerce. That to that end it is necessary that our coaling-stations and harbours shall be adequately armed and garrisoned, and that the garrisons of our distant stations beyond sea shall be permanently maintained there; because war breaks out always with such startling rapidity that garrisons not on the spot are useless, while our Foreign Office will, beyond all doubt, resist, as a matter of diplomatic prudence, reinforcement on the eve of war, even if war ever had a really long " eve." The only time when we can garrison Hong-Kong, Singapore, and the like, is during profound peace.

In the first article of the consecutive series, called " Russia and England," I have maintained—

having here very powerful support from Sir Charles Dilke's arguments—that two facts have changed altogether for us the circumstances with which other generations of Englishmen had to deal. The first of these is this, that the frontiers of Russia and England now virtually march side by side in Asia. The second is, that the armed forces of Continental Powers have been developed to an extent of which most Englishmen have never formed to themselves any conception at all. I have appealed to evidence, which I believe to be unanswerable, to prove that we can never make terms with Russia to which Russia will adhere longer than it suits her.

Just at this moment, when Russia has objects and purposes which clash with the wishes and interests of Continental Powers, she will be sure to be most willing to arrange terms which will for the time keep us quiet. She is not actually ready to attack us in India. We know that she intends to do so. Of course, if she can divide us from others whom she wishes to crush also, she will do it. "*Divide et Impera*" is not a maxim which is brannew in 1888.

My contention in this article is that, if we can act in such a way that we can lend effective service to other Powers who have an interest in opposing the designs of Russia in Europe, and if we can make that service so valuable that it would be worth their while to make with us a treaty which would equally prohibit Russian attack on India, it is our true policy to do so.

Furthermore, I have shown that the territorial conditions of our Indian frontier greatly increase the importance of this question. It is vitally important to stop Russia from possessing herself of the Heri Rud. For reasons I have given, we cannot safely attempt this from India. It is not there that "land and sea much intertwine."

The remaining articles all deal with the question thus raised.

In the second—that headed "Germany, France, and Belgium"—I have endeavoured to show, by comparing the conditions of foreign Powers on the Continent and our own, that those statesmen are leading us on to a false scent who, acknowledging the necessity which the present time presents for a more effective condition of our armaments, believe that they may at the same time reduce our expenditure, because, as they say, foreign Powers do so much more with a given sum of money than we do.

It is difficult to keep the bearing of an argument, carried on in consecutive months, before readers who do not necessarily read each article. I was therefore not surprised that a few critics, who admitted the truth of what I said, made also some complaint that I should connect this subject of relative expense with that of the "Balance of

Power in Europe." Now it will be observed that the problem I set myself was to discuss the question raised by Lord Wolseley and Sir Fitz-James Stephen's Commission, the importance of which had been admitted by Sir Charles Dilke—"What we want, what we want it for, and whether we can afford to pay for it." My dealing with "The Balance of Power in Europe" is an all-important incident of the reply to that question, because I contend that the present condition of the balance of power in Europe determines how we can most economically and effectively develop and employ our power for the defence of the Empire. But it is obvious also, that the question whether we can for the same money obtain the results secured by foreign Powers is also an essential element of my answer. I believe that I have shown reason for my contention that our own army is incomparably the cheapest army in the world, in the sense that, for the work it does, it puts less strain upon the country, and takes less money out of it, than the army of any Continental State. I am far from contending that no reforms are needed. I believe they are. But I believe that they must be reforms which assume the conditions of English life, and do not ignore them. So far from wishing to modify anything I have said in this part of the article, I desire to reinforce it by two remarks I have not there made.

Introduction. xix

First, there is only one country in the world which fairly compares with our own in expenditure. The United States alone of all countries has, like our own, the commercial wisdom to pay directly for what it wants.

Now the great anomaly on which would-be economical reformers fasten, as the extravagant fact connected with our army, is, that with a force of 208,357 regulars we have a non-effective return of nearly *three million pounds sterling.*

Now the United States army consists of 25,000 men, all told. Its non-effective return reaches *seventeen million pounds sterling.*

As I am anxious to emphasise this fact, and do not wish to be supposed to have made some mistake as to currency, I will put it also that it costs *eighty million of dollars.*

Of course that is largely a result of the great Civil War; but that does not affect the point for which I mention it—namely, that it may happen that a non-effective return represents some of the best money that is paid by a country. I have shown in the text what the services are which our non-effective return renders us in one respect; but as, since my articles were written, a great point has been made about the extravagance of our medical non-effective return, and as the facts on that subject supply some instructive information, I shall touch on it here.

The reason why our medical pension-list is so high is this. A few years ago the Government and the medical schools were at war. The schools beat the Government hip and thigh, from Dan to Beersheba. In utter despair of getting any medical men for the army, the Government surrendered at discretion. It appeared possible to take advantage of the conditions of medical civil life in England in this way. Young doctors usually spend the first seven years or so of their medical life in getting old enough to be supposed fit to take up a practice, spending that time on merchant-ships, in attending hospitals, or in various ways which for the most part are somewhat disjointed from their after-career. It was thought, and it has proved true, that by offering a lump sum at stated periods early in their career, or small pensions a little later, the ablest young doctors might be tempted to enter the army for a time, without sacrificing the more lucrative prospects of civil practice. Now it is to be observed that if this scheme succeeded, its inevitable effect would be to increase the medical "non-effective return" out of proportion to the "effective return." The pensions were, in fact, the very means by which the Government paid for the services of the men actually in the army. As they induced abler men to join the service than could be obtained in any other way because of the conditions of civil practice, and as they induced them to accept relatively low rates of pay, there is nothing in the mere fact of the large "non-effective medical return," which of itself proves that we are not obtaining our doctors by the cheapest scheme on which we can get them. Whether it may or may not be better to pay in some other way, I am not concerned to discuss. But I am certain that the outcry against the mere circumstance of the high relation between the medical "non-effective" and the "effective" return—that is, between the proportions paid for pensions and for pay to doctors in the army—is merely and only the result of ignorance of the facts, or of short memories. It is startling to find that, of all the statesmen who were members of the House of Commons when these arrangements were made, no one remembers them sufficiently well to be able conclusively to answer a purely fictitious though most plausible cry. All is *not* gold that glitters; but we are always being run away with by glitter, because no one scratches below the surface. The chances at present are that, yielding to an outcry, the weakness of which they do not take the trouble to examine, our statesmen may be forced into a fresh trial of strength with the medical schools. They will infallibly be beaten, and will have to make probably yet more ignominious terms with their triumphant conquerers. "Their triumphant conquerers" think of it. Imagine these words applied to the Governments of Germany, Austria, and Russia, and then gravely discuss the question of the money you vote for your army, and the money they vote. In Germany the medical man is under the compulsion which the general conditions of universal service put upon him. He is glad enough to be employed on his proper work, to go through a Government school which offers him educational facilities, binding himself to serve afterwards as a medical man on cheap terms. But blink the matter as they may, that compulsion is itself an enormous money-tax inflicted on the profession as a whole. It appears in no budget. Yet the general effect is to extract from the country, though it comes from only one section of it, an enormously larger sum than we pay for our medical service.

It is strangely difficult to get people to look at a question from a point of view to which they are not accustomed. Because I was contending in this article that, great as in many respects were the services which universal military training renders to the health and order of a country, it is very dear as a mere question of money, I was in one quarter answered, "No one thinks of introducing universal service. You waste your breath in arguing against it." I am not arguing against it at all. I am simply accepting our conditions as they stand, and I say that our budget, ugly as it *looks*, is in fact so small a one as compared with the concealed money waste of universal service, that our people are deceived by its appearance. Everybody says that, if only the country were convinced that it is getting its money's worth for its money, it would gladly do what is necessary for national security. I maintain, and no one has yet faced my argument, that we get our army more cheaply than any other Power; that here and there economies may be effected, but that the broad fact remains that the thirty-eight millions will barely maintain our home and Indian army in current efficiency, and that the additional sums we require for horses, stores, effective armaments, garrisons for coaling-stations and harbours, and for an efficient navy, cannot be obtained without exceptional expenditure, such as all Continental Powers have incurred for them. Direct money payment for each thing you want is, as every one who has ever catered for bar or army mess, or for a party of any other body of men, knows by experience, the most thrifty mode of payment. But thrift may become ruinous if the large figures staring you in the face frighten you from paying what is necessary for efficiency, because others who pay through the nose without realising it, don't face figures as large.

The medical case is a capital illustration, because it is the one instance in which the Government comes fairly face to face with the professional conditions of a wealthy country. These conditions tell, nevertheless, in directions where they are not known to tell. All through my service I have hardly known any very able men in the army who, unless very wealthy, were not continually being forced to consider whether they could afford to remain in it. Of course in many instances they yield to necessity, and a disastrous process of weeding goes on. This process, which drives able men out of the army, is continually working. The temptations which are held out to them in England are enormous. I could give case after case of the most startling kind. It applies to all ranks. In some instances I could clearly show the direct pecuniary loss which has resulted to the country from the fact of the tremendous competition offered by civil life. When large English companies find it commercially advantageous to pay their chairman £7500 per annum, as is the case with one large railway company, £8000 per annum, as is the case with others, it is absurd to say, as the cry now is, that the pay of our highest civil and military servants is to be compared with those of Germany. I am certain that the direction in which economy is being looked for is a false one. Not one question is asked by any Parliamentary or other committee with the view to ascertain these facts. Nay, when any evidence is tendered which may possibly show that economy lies in a different

Introduction. xxv

direction from that which is assumed, it is usually ignored and neglected. Now you cannot really secure economy except by facing facts. Inquiry, the object of which is not to ascertain truth but to confirm an established popular prejudice, will certainly lead to conclusions which end in disaster.

Therefore I am certain that the discussion in the pages of this volume, 69-96, on "German and English Economy," is a necessary and a most important part of the inquiry with which I am here concerned. I am happy to find from the notices, more especially in the leading provincial papers, that hardly any has excited more interest, or has been more generally confirmed from local experience, some papers having supplied fresh facts of the greatest value bearing on the matter. I have reason to know that Lord Randolph Churchill has had some unpleasant experiences in trying to press his views on men of large commercial knowledge.

The next subject—that of the military frontiers of France and Germany—is intended, first, to serve the purpose of assisting readers to understand the general situation between those Powers, so as to follow with an intelligent interest discussions which are daily appearing in the newspapers, and to understand events if war should unhappily break out. Secondly, it is necessary as part of the account of the general situation of Europe, in order to show how our power can be most economically exerted for our own defence. The questions about Belgium, and our relations to that country, so obviously concern ourselves, that I do not think they need be further touched on here.

In the article on "Germany, Russia, and Austria," the same double purpose is followed. The final article deals with the whole situation as it concerns ourselves. Its purpose is to show that the rise of the Italian power has offered us the opportunity of affording that assistance to the Continental Powers which will enable us, on the *do ut des* principle, to secure that alliance the advantage of which it was the object of the first article to insist upon.

The anonymous veil that was originally thrown over the authorship of these articles was always very thin. I never concealed my identity from any one who cared to know it. Sir Charles Dilke was informed of my purpose before I published an article, because I was naturally unwilling to attack him without letting him know who his assailant was. Nevertheless it has had one useful effect. Despite the extreme kindness which I have met with from most of my critics, a few have illustrated rather amusingly their ideas and experiences as to the anonymous in writing. As they are most of them anonymous writers, the facts are suggestive.

I had warmly defended the proper use of cavalry, quoting the names of the greatest authorities in

Europe as guarantees for the truth of what I had said. Therefore one critic announced, without hesitation, that I was a cavalry officer. I had spoken of General Brackenbury as "one of the most distinguished of living artillery officers," therefore another critic announced in three successive paragraphs, as a fact within his own knowledge, that I was General Brackenbury. It is needless to say that, having this exact knowledge of my identity, he displayed his literary critical capacity by detecting in parts of these articles a style identical with certain other articles which, as he alleged, General Brackenbury had written.

I presume that it was in vengeance for his error that he, the week after he had discovered it, proceeded to attack "military professors"—it being obvious that two years' special study at the Staff College in an official appointment, which I received on the understanding that it would in no way interfere with my employment on active service, had changed my nature as a soldier after four campaigns and twenty-four years' previous service in the army.

The same critic assumed that it was because of some salaries in which I was specially interested, that I pointed out that, for instance, the Portsmouth command, the pay of which is unusually large, is only an expense to its holder, and does not in the proper sense yield pay at all.

The one thing which these gentlemen seem unable to conceive is, that there are some of us, whose business it has been to watch events closely for some years past, not from a party point of view, but in the interest of national safety, who really and earnestly believe that there are facts which it is vital that the country should face. I myself know from many conversations that even the most intelligent classes in this country are not in the least aware of the actual condition of the armed Powers of the Continent. Sir Wilfrid Lawson is able to say to an average audience without being hissed, "Why should not we invade France instead of France invading us, if we have a Channel Tunnel?" And the depth of the folly which that sentence expresses is not understood by one Englishman in ten among business men or professional men.

Now we soldiers may be all wrong in what we say. Those who are not soldiers or sailors may be the only people who can think without bias—who can judge what ought to be done. But no men of any kind can be right who form their conclusions from false assumptions as to facts. What I find everywhere is that the facts which may be gathered [1]

---

[1] Alack! I had in my haste written, "say from the 'Statesman's Year-Book,'" but reference at once showed that that work was deceptive, and deceptive only and completely, as to the strength of armies. English statesmen "care for none of these things," and those who cater for them know it.

from any authoritative source altogether independent of soldiers are not known, and, as Mr Gladstone once put it in an analogous matter, "If they are read, they are not marked, learned, and inwardly digested."

I do not know how the facts are to be brought home if it is assumed at once and without examination of what he says, that whoever has been obliged to look into these facts must necessarily have some secret base motive for asking his countrymen to examine them. Surely the question is sufficiently serious—I do not mean by that panic-suggesting, but merely not fitting for a society journal joke—to make it right that some men who cannot have any base motive, such as these writers instantly attribute to a soldier or sailor, should look for themselves into the question and see whether these things are so or not.

Perhaps I may now claim that, by the very assumptions which these writers have made as to my probable identity, I come forward under circumstances which do not suggest the presumption of prejudice. A soldier, I am pleading before all things for the navy. I am pleading on grounds of the military study of the Continent, which it has belonged to my office to undertake, and which I think I have made intelligible to the mind of all Englishmen, so that they who are not soldiers or sailors may judge for themselves.

Trained and militarily bred as a field-artilleryman, and having had the honour of wearing the Horse-Artillery jacket, I am, from sheer conviction, pleading that, for the sake of the country, we field-gunners must bear to see our own arm reduced, rather than that the army as a whole, including the artillery, should not be able to act with the promptitude which is necessary for the service of the country.

I am pleading thus, though I know that our Volunteers and militia stand sorely in need of the support of field-guns, and that they are not an army without them.

I am pleading thus against a most brilliant writer, who has given more study to foreign armies than any other of our statesmen, and who girds at me because I do not believe it possible on our present estimates to make an increase of 390, or, as he at first not unfairly urged as the proper complement, 900 field-guns.

Perhaps the generous critics to whom I have alluded may discover for me the hidden baseness which may lead me to suggest that the money required for this object ought first to be spent in ensuring the safety of our harbours and coaling-stations—in none of which I hope ever to be employed—and in ensuring the supremacy of our navy, in which I have no other concern than that of a tax-payer and a subject of the English crown.

The increase of the field-artillery would, in fact, have for me the most direct and immediate professional advantage. It would give to me under almost any possible organisation such professional advancement as would be of more value to me than any other merely personal advantage that an expenditure of money can bring. I do not think, therefore, that the pleas I put forward ought, from the mere source from which they spring, to be met with suspicion.

The audience to which I am anxious to appeal are the lawyers, the business men, the doctors, the numbers of intelligent working men whom I know to be interested in the concerns of their country. Of course I am glad to have the support of soldiers as to the military soundness of what I have urged. I can hardly receive kinder, warmer, or more authoritative testimony on that point than I have received. But unless Englishmen generally will judge for themselves of the policy I here advocate, my words are wasted. Statesmen cannot, for the reasons I have assigned, make for us that federal treaty which, as I believe, will ensure peace in our generation, will protect India and secure our commerce; still less can they ensure the efficiency of our small army and the necessary supremacy of our navy without your support, sir, or madam, who chance to be reading this. It is in proportion as the nation refuses by practical voting to allow the question of our foreign policy to be made the shuttlecock of party, that foreign statesmen are ready to give as we give. I am speaking on some of the very best authority in all Europe when I so speak. You can play your part in making the question intelligible to others. In its broad outline it is a very simple one, and easily explained. The Secretary of the Treasury is your representative. It is to save your pocket that he turns out Lord Charles Beresford. He does so merely because we, none of us, like to pay what is needed to make the navy efficient. I have as little liking for the tax-gatherer's little chit as you have. I have no more personal interest in the navy than you. But I have had to study matters which, if you will follow these pages, you may understand as well as I do. If you do understand them, you will see that every shilling we now save in taxes from Treasury decisions, which help to make the navy inefficient, is ruinous extravagance. We shall have to live a very few years in order to pay for them in many pounds for each shilling, and we shall then have suffered in a thousand other ways which no pounds will redeem.

It was—as Mr Kinglake has shown without a possible logical flaw, on the evidence of exhaustive Parliamentary inquiries—the direct act of a Secretary of the Treasury, Sir Charles Trevelyan, which absolutely caused all the misery, the extravagance, and the loss of life of the Crimean Winter. There is no man living who, for the reasons I have named, is so directly your representative and mine as taxpayers as the Permanent Secretary of the Treasury. It is as you feel that he will act. If you choose to have such a navy and an army so mobile that you can by their aid ensure the support of the Central Powers in keeping Russia quiet, Sir Reginald Welby will not be a second Sir Charles Trevelyan.[1] You will have no war with Russia for India at all, in all human probability. At the worst, if you do, it will be a short one, for you will have some of the greatest Powers in the world on your side. There are few facts more certain in the world than that within the next ten years the fruits of your decision will have been gathered. The one thing on which you must not reckon is, that any one in the position of the Secretary of the Treasury will take them into account. They never have done in all their history, and they never will. The question that concerns them is the preparation of the Budget of the year. The Budgets of the next ten years are beyond their purview.

I have had occasion to refer several times to the scheme for the British army apparently suggested by Sir Charles Dilke. My reference has been al-

---

[1] The offices are not identical, though both are correctly described as Secretaries of the Treasury. The distinction is irrelevant to my purpose.

ways to these words: "I am convinced that by an expenditure of far less than the 36 to 38 millions sterling which we spend already upon our army, we could create a force which would make our enemies pause before they ventured to attack us. This is not the time to work out, as I intend to do, the possible relations in the new infantry system between what might be called the guards, the militia, and the volunteers. Some of the Australian colonies, in their new military systems, have recognised the distinction which should exist, in order to call out the full local military strength, between various classes of what they style volunteers. Some of them have a force in the nature of a volunteer militia which is paid, . . . and it will be interesting at a future time to consider whether the various Australian military systems do not point out to us the way in which we should walk in future."[1]

I think I was justified in concluding from these words, accompanied by a fierce attack upon all the steps actually being taken to give us two effective army corps and a cavalry division, that Sir Charles Dilke did not realise the importance of "our amphibious strength." The desire to bring home to all men the importance to England of possessing a highly mobile force, helped to make me wish to lay before them the facts which are here recorded.

[1] 'Present Position of European Politics,' pp. 333, 334.

Sir Charles Dilke, in his more recent articles, has declared his wish to provide us with the two army corps and a cavalry division, and has cited the case of Switzerland to show that we ought to be able also to possess several hundred field-guns. As he has withdrawn from the proposal to reduce our expenditure, and now, on the contrary, thinks that we must increase it, I naturally can only await with unalloyed interest the explanation of his present proposals. I have no reason to suppose that they will clash with anything that I have here said. They certainly will not tend, if they carry out the indications he has now given, to diminish the importance of what I have urged.

The system of a developed militia, which the original proposal appeared to suggest, met its *coup de grâce* at Olmutz in 1849. So long as we get the power which will, on the *do ut des* principle, enable us to play our part in keeping the peace of Europe, and in keeping Russia out of India, I am content.

NOTE.

I HAVE on the whole preferred to retain the articles in their original form, only putting in such matters as would bring them up to date. To distinguish between the new notes added to the volume and the original text and notes, I have retained the "we" of the originals, but have written "I" in the notes added afterwards.

THE
BALANCE OF MILITARY POWER IN EUROPE.

It is a curious fact that the most unmistakable mark of himself which it appears likely that Mr Bright will leave behind him on our Statute-book is to be found in the Army Act. Up to the year 1867 the preamble of the Mutiny Act had always declared that the purpose for which the army was maintained was "the safety of the United Kingdom, the defence of the possessions of her Majesty's crown, and the preservation of the balance of power in Europe."

But when Mr Bright became a Cabinet Minister in Mr Gladstone's Administration, the words referring to the "balance of power in Europe" were, at his instance, dropped out; and as the preamble to the annual Act now stands, our army exists only for "the safety of the United Kingdom and the defence of the possessions of her Majesty's crown."

As a rule, abstract questions, such for instance as the purposes for which we maintain armed forces at all, are not in England thrashed out. A writer here or there propounds a theory which obtains a certain amount of acceptance; and a few years later one finds it taken for granted by the careless and the thoughtless that certain assumptions, on which no adequate Areopagus has ever decided, are to be accepted for the future as the primary data of all discussion. Then some fine morning a Cabinet Minister gives practical effect to the abstract discussion, and we discover that the reasonings which appeared to be too little serious to need the attention of men absorbed by everyday work, have had the most momentous effect on practical politics at least, if not on business and life.

Mr Bright, then, has duly dismissed to the shades the wicked dream of our great statesmen of the past, that it was not for the wellbeing of England that any one Power on the Continent should assume a position so preponderating that it could dictate tyrannically to all its neighbours. History would appear to confirm the view that for any State to acquire, as Spain did under Charles and Philip, or France did under Louis XIV. and Napoleon, or as Russia did under Nicholas, a position of overweening power, is a matter dangerously affecting the liberties of nations. In former days our statesmen thought that, for the safety of England herself, she ought to be ready to join hands with other nations in defending the liberties of Europe. They believed that nations, like individuals, have their duties as well as their rights, and that the neglect of one, or carelessness in regard to the other, is sure, sooner or later, to meet with punishment. They embodied these ideas in the phrase, "the balance of power in Europe." It may or may not have been a happy one. We have no anxiety to see it restored to the preamble of the Army Act. Still it had its advantages. It avoided all terms of pharisaical assumption, yet it declared to other nations our readiness to play some other than a purely selfish part. It naturally made them ready to meet us on the *do ut des* principle—the principle, that is, of mutual co-operation for national independence. But what we cannot help noting with some amusement is the quaint humour with which, in these matters, Time brings his revenges. Here, in the month of June 1887, we have a writer of the extremest Radical school concluding a series of articles—on what? Well, he says they are on "The Position of European Politics." But, we call Mr Bright himself to witness that we are setting down nought in malice, —"the trail of the serpent is over them all." "The balance of power in Europe" is the subject with which this very able writer finds himself at every turn compelled to deal. Dismissed from the preamble of the Mutiny Act, it forces itself into practical politics from the moment politics cease to be insular—that is, from the moment that, in guiding the helm of the State, the pilot does not sleep, and, sleeping, dream that he can escape all storms because he sees none that are rising.

We have recently had from three distinct quarters an earnest demand that the country shall really make up its mind for what purposes it maintains its military forces, and what those forces are expected to do. Differing on nearly every other subject, the Fortnightly Reviewer and the Adjutant-General of the Army [1] are agreed in this, that it is utterly impossible that we can have our armed forces on a satisfactory footing until some authoritative body determines what we ought to expect from them. In so far as Sir James Fitz-James Stephen's Commission has had opportunity, it has earnestly pressed upon us the same sound principle.

It has been noticed already by some of those who have criticised the work of the Fortnightly Reviewer, that he has strangely ignored the conditions under which modern armies engage; and that, whether his statistical calculations of numeri-

---

[1] The reference is to the article contributed by Lord Wolseley to the Jubilee Volume edited by Mr Ward.

cal force be accurate or not, his balance is not a true balance, because he treats the value of a soldier as a quantity absolutely independent of all his fighting qualities and national characteristics. Yet Napoleon was in the habit of reckoning the elements of the forces with which he dealt, for practical purposes and as a matter of business, on the principle that a man of one nationality might be taken as the equivalent of so many more of another. Whatever was the case in his day, it is perfectly certain that in ours a mass of men incapable of acting so as effectively to use modern arms becomes simply a broader target for shot as its numbers increase. Moreover, the writer throughout treats force, latent somewhere or other in a country, as though that could be reckoned as the actually available fighting-power on the battlefield. He laughs, not without some justice, in his final article—that on England—at Mr Howard Vincent for speaking of the ultimate forces of the British empire as 2,250,000 men, " without telling us anything of the time that it would take to place even a tenth of this force in line near London." Yet in the article on Russia, he himself does precisely the same thing as regards the Russian forces. He treats the vast numbers of armed Russians available somewhere or other among the great deserts and mountains and roadless morasses of Russia, as though they had all to be reckoned with on the frontiers of Germany and Austria whenever it pleased the Tzar to issue his fiat that they should move thither. He complains that those who dispute the accuracy of the picture he has drawn of the colossus of the north do not appreciate the improvement that has taken place in the Russian army since the Turkish war of 1877-78, yet he utterly fails to show how the weaknesses which then existed have been remedied. He gives no hint that he is aware how amazing was the weakness which Russia actually displayed in the Turkish campaign; and indeed in some parts of his latest article, when he is having his wicked will of the "Jingoes,"—a safe pastime always for a Radical politician in distress,—he demonstrates absolutely that he either does not know it, or finds it convenient for the purposes of his argument to suppress the fact.

Holding, therefore, with the Fortnightly Reviewer, Sir James Fitz-James Stephen's Commission, and the Adjutant-General, that it is of vital consequence for us to determine in military matters "what we want," what we want it for, and whether we can afford to pay for it, we propose, in the following pages, to discuss the military relations of the great Powers of the Continent at the present moment, and to consider how far those relations affect our own military power. We propose to take up those precise aspects of the question which have been altogether ignored by the Reviewer. We purpose not only to study the armed forces of the Continent, as they exist on paper, as well as our own, but we intend further to take account of the medium in which those forces have necessarily to interact. That is to say, we mean to allow for the influence of those conditions of modern warfare, conformity to the laws of which determines what the effective fighting-power of nations really is, almost as much as any numerical estimate of their fighting men can possibly determine it. We are convinced that the whole tendency of the articles which have dealt with the "Position of Modern Politics" has been to put these matters in a false light. We are sure that their writer would have us believe that England is weak where she is strong, and strong where she is weak, and that he has misjudged the other forces among which her power has to act. In particular, as regards Russia, he has, as we believe, put her strength for weakness, and her weakness for strength. He has not taken account of the effect upon the position of England in Europe of the rise of the new power Italy, whose army and politics he has in many respects most admirably described. He has in many most important respects misjudged the strength of Austria, of Germany, and of France. In almost every instance, not from an inaccurate statement of bare facts, so far as he has given them, but from assumptions radically false, he has tended to lead our statesmen astray. We therefore look upon it as a duty, for the sake of our national future, to endeavour, whilst there is yet time, to remove the false impressions which have been produced on the minds of men by these attractive papers.

For the most part, we shall state our own convictions, and the grounds on which they are based. We shall not weary our readers with lengthy controversy. Indeed we shall have little need to do so. The writer, as a rule, deals only in dogmatic assertion on military matters. He is sure, for instance, that the French frontier and the Russian frontier against Germany are much stronger than the German against either. He gives no grounds for his assertion, and he does not describe the character of the frontiers. We hope to be able to make clear to all our readers our reasons for believing the precise contrary.[1] He is sure that on military grounds the Germans will march through Belgium; he is sure that England will not resist them if they do. We deny the soundness of his military assumption, and we propose to expose the weakness of the grounds of his political one. We intend, in either case, to state fully the reasons for our belief.[2]

---

[1] See II., "Germany, France, and Belgium;" and III., "Germany, Russia, and Austria."

[2] See II., "Germany, France, and Belgium."

This part of the subject—that of relative military power, and of the courses of action which are, as a consequence of it, open to us—is of such paramount importance, and needs such full statement, that we cannot follow him into those deeply interesting, but—may we say it without offence?—slightly gossipy records of past politics which have enlivened his pages.

We must, however, once and for all, enter our protest against the claim of the writer to appeal to those who desire to put aside "personal and party prejudice." Whether or not he "who drives fat oxen should himself be fat," this much at least is certain, that the appeal to men to judge, on higher than party grounds, questions in which party passions have been largely involved, can only justly be made by a man who first takes the beam out of his own eye. In our life, among all the passionate perversions of facts, of which we have had enough and more than enough of late years, we have never read assumptions as to the past more grotesquely unfair than those which are thus paraded under the banner of impartial history. For a man with the past political record of Sir Charles Dilke, who has now avowed the authorship of these papers, to attempt, when writing anonymously, and at a time when his identity was really concealed, to pass for an impartial historian, weighing, with the fair balance and even weight of one looking only to his country's good, the foreign policy of the past, seems to us, to put it mildly, to be a not very ingenuous proceeding. But in every historical statement, still more in every carefully considered omission, the cloven foot of the bitter partisan peeps out. It is made worse, not better, by the well-calculated compliment to Lord Salisbury's recent policy, so worded as to make it appear as though Lord Salisbury had done little more than adopt Lord Rosebery's line of action in foreign affairs, so that it matters now little which party is in office, so far as foreign politics are concerned. There is something strangely cynical in this boundless faith in the short memory of the English public.

It happens that, in one particular instance, we are anxious to recall a passage of past history which it has suited Sir Charles Dilke's purpose to forget. Our purpose in recalling it is, however, to illustrate the form in which the power of England can now be most effectively employed. We only incidentally touch on the historical error.

It has pleased Sir Charles Dilke to fix the date when that reign of force began in Europe, which, as he truly says, now so determines facts, that every politician of the present day who desires to be more than a vestryman, must understand the conditions under which armies are marshalled for the field. We allege distinctly that he has fixed that date solely, we will not say for the purposes of party, but blinded to the plainest historical facts by that spirit of partisanship which, after years of party life, has become to him a second nature, from which he can no more emancipate himself than he can leap from his own shadow. He says that England, at the Berlin Congress, contributed to set up that reign of force because we "virtually annexed an island which had not been conquered," and that from that moment the reign of force began. We say that England did contribute her share to the setting up the reign of force in Europe, but that it was not in the year 1878, when, with the full assent of the Sultan of Turkey, we occupied Cyprus. The reign of blood and iron was not established by paying good gold that might have enabled reforms to be carried out, and by actually improving the administration of a Turkish island. No! It was in the month of February 1864 that England, after—through the mouth of Lord Kimberley, then Lord Wodehouse—she had persuaded the Danes to surrender to Prussian aggression the first line of their defences and the fortress of Rendsburg, expressly on the ground that, till that was done, she could afford no material assistance, drew back and left the Danish monarchy to be dismembered avowedly by sheer force.[1]

[1] No doubt at all times *force* has been the only means by which

Nothing in all diplomacy is recorded with more precision than the fact that then force was set up as the rule of right. The Berlin lawyers expressly recorded their opinion after the war that Prussia and Austria were the sole lawful possessors of the Duchies, because the *only original right* to them was that of the reigning King of Denmark, who, as a consequence of the conquest, had transferred by treaty all his rights in them to the conquering States.[1]

Of the part which England played in those transactions, the father of the present ambassador in Berlin, Sir A. Malet, has, in his 'Overthrow of the Germanic Confederation,' recorded his view in terms of such vigour as a diplomatist rarely permits himself. He has shown conclusively that England did lead the Danes to suppose that armed assistance would be offered by her, even if she stood alone. It was, in fact, certain that

---

law could be *enforced*. It is almost tautology to say so. What I contend is that, from the fall of Napoleon onwards up to 1864, there had been an acknowledged principle that the "European concert" should resist the exercise of mere force. Rightly or wrongly, our statesmen in 1864 believed that force was being wrongfully exercised, and yielded to it. I have myself always had great sympathy with the German determination not to allow Germans to be bullied. Our action was based on no such feeling, but on sheer fear of redeeming our pledged word. Either it was wrong to pledge our word, or it was wrong not to redeem it. What I desire to show is that we could have redeemed it.

[1] See a very clear summary of this remarkable State paper in the Annual Register for 1865. Foreign History, p. 245.

she would not stand alone. Austria knew well that Prussia was then preparing her overthrow, and she was therefore only waiting for a signal from us to abandon the artificial alliance into which she had been forced. The French Emperor was only sulking because we had refused to join him in his proposed European Congress. The feeling in France in behalf of the Danes would have been too strong to be long resisted. Sweden with her gallant little army was ready to join us at once. All that was needed was the facing of a momentary danger of enormous apparent magnitude.

We have always believed that, in a military sense, the danger was apparent only. We speak on the evidence of some of the best trained English soldiers who were actually present at the struggle, when we say that we believe that, had even such a force as we could then have sent to Denmark been joined to the Danish and Swedish armies, positions could in that most peculiar country have been taken up where, protected by the guns of our fleets, the united army, all of excellent quality, could have defied the utmost efforts of the Austro-Prussian forces to break down their resistance. It needed only a few weeks of boldly facing the risk then, to have broken down the first avowed effort at setting up the law of force in Europe.

We are far from saying that we now wish all

the history of the past undone. We are by no means sure that the formation of a United Germany in the centre of Europe, by whatever means it has been brought about, has not been the event of our time which in the long-run will most tend to the happiness of the human race. But that England then, for the first time, shrank back from redeeming her virtually pledged word in the presence of mere force, and that she did so under a mistaken estimate of her danger, we are firmly convinced. We believe that then Prussia, despite her breech-loaders, which she had not tried in war, and with an army organisation which, inaugurated only four years before, was not as yet complete, would have evaded the struggle, knowing well the dangers to which in a short time she would have been exposed.

What Sir Alexander Malet does not record, but what is nevertheless a matter of history, is that the great question on which the whole future of European history, "of the position of European politics," for at least a century, of the "balance of European power" was to depend, was settled at a certain Cabinet Council in London. Then for the first—not for the last—time the Sibyl presented herself to the responsible statesmen of England, offering for a price, not, as she did to Tarquin, merely the books which should foretell the future, but ready at their bidding to change the very course of history. Before that Cabinet Council, Lord Palmerston and Lord Russell had been conscious of the absolute obligation which lay upon England to redeem words which, taken in their natural meaning by those to whom they were addressed, were now pleaded by Denmark as binding us to support her. They had actually ordered Sir Alfred Horsford to prepare the scheme for an English army to be landed on the shores of Denmark, though for the moment we should have had alone to face two of the great Powers of the Continent. But when the Cabinet Council broke up, Sir Alfred Horsford heard no more of any warlike proposals.

Who had carried the decision of the Council in the teeth of two such statesmen? Who had succeeded in persuading an English Cabinet to make itself responsible for the true inauguration of the reign of Blood and Iron? Who had triumphed so far over all the past traditions of English policy? Who had set the ball a-rolling which, with rapid rush, was to lead on to the "overthrow of the Germanic Confederation," to the annexation of Alsace-Lorraine, to the creation of that life of war in peace-time which now lies like a blight on all the nations of the Continent?

It has not needed that the Queen's secrets should be betrayed in order that it should be matter of notoriety that in that Cabinet meeting, though other influences affected the question, and though other members of the Cabinet were strongly in favour of a peace policy, that which decided it was the overmastering eloquence of Mr Gladstone.

It is not therefore surprising that a Radical statesman who up to the last associated himself with the very latest phases of what Mr Bright has lately called "Mr Gladstone's many turnings of his coat," should desire to forget that very noteworthy date of February 1864, and should desire to transfer to the Congress of Berlin the responsibility for that change in English politics and in the international law of Europe which was then inaugurated. It is not unnatural, we say, that he should "desire" to make this change. But, seeing that all that we have here written is known to Sir Charles Dilke as well as it is to us, with what face, when he thus changes some of the best-known pages of history in accordance with partisan desires, can he address himself "to those, if there be such in these days, who are free from party prejudice, from prejudice personal and national—to those, in short, who try to see things as they really are"? That is certainly what we wish to do, as far as we can; but we are warned by the example of the Reviewer against protesting too much.

It is by no means only with a view to the question of the correct date of the origin of the modern reign of force that we have referred to the story of the Danish war. The chief purpose for which we recall it to mind will appear fully after we have dealt with a very curious confession, accompanied, as we do not think but absolutely know, by an enormous historical error of fact, of the gravest possible consequence.

"If," says Sir Charles Dilke, "I have sometimes fallen foul of those whom I look upon as belonging to the Jingo school of 1878, it is because I doubt their wisdom. Of their patriotism I have a profound conviction; and it is only of their methods that I complain, believing as I do that the inflated language of 1878 was a mere insult to our intelligence, and that the occupation of Cyprus was a blunder calculated to divert the country from the penitential consideration of its own real military weakness, and of the true ways in which that weakness should be remedied. . . . Nevertheless I hate to contend with them, because I feel all the time that upon the essential points we are in real agreement,—namely, that we are living in a fool's paradise; that we are not in a military position, in spite of the enormous sums that we have been spending, to defend the empire against attack."[1]

Now there is a good deal here which suggests food for reflection. To begin with, the word

[1] Present Position of European Politics, pp. 330, 331.

"Jingo"[1] is one of extremely doubtful acceptation. It was originally invented by Mr Bradlaugh, and made its first appearance, under his auspices, in a letter which appeared in the 'Daily News,' in which he said that a certain race of people had recently come to be known "whom *I* call Jingoes." The word was eagerly caught at, at the time, by Mr Gladstone's followers, because there existed, independently of party, a widespread feeling of patriotic appreciation of the position which, under Lord Beaconsfield's guidance, England had assumed in Europe, and it was necessary, for party purposes, to pour contempt upon that feeling.

In all such popular movements there are necessarily elements of vulgarity mixed, and the music-hall song which was popular at the time expressed undoubtedly the vulgar side of the feeling in the words—

> "For we don't want to fight,
> But, *by Jingo*, if we do,
> We've got the ships, we've got the men,
> We've got the money too."

Shortly afterwards Sir William Vernon Harcourt, at Oxford, fully explained what he and his friends meant by flinging the expression "Jingoes" at those who differed from them in opinion. He began by saying, "Do you want to know who the

---

[1] We speak, of course, of the political nickname, and not of the ancient oath.

Jingoes are? I will tell you who they are." And then, using that ample vituperative vocabulary with which he is supplied, he proceeded to represent a character in which everything that was contemptible in point of brains, loathsome in point of vice, repulsive in manners, was mingled in a well-chosen mass of offensiveness.

From this time onwards, therefore, the word served two purposes, different in degree but similar in kind, and both of them invaluable. In the first place, the name was of a meaning sufficiently uncertain to prevent it, in its apparent use, from being too manifestly abusive for the purposes of ordinary conversation. "Oh, you are a Jingo!" was in 1880 the ready reply to any one who thought that Mr Gladstone was a man capable of human error, or that Lord Beaconsfield might occasionally slide, by accident, into conduct which was neither that of a fool nor of a knave. To all who so far in either respect transgressed the party creed of the passing hour, the expression was so used, no matter what their antecedents might have been. It was intended to hint, without asserting that it would necessarily follow, that the person so addressed was probably an habitual frequenter of the lowest music-halls in London, and that it was quite an open point whether, properly speaking, all that Sir William Vernon Harcourt had said of him was not true.

Thus the word was delightful alike in the universal sweep with which it could be flung, in its deliberate and essential insolence of purpose, and in its vagueness. When, therefore, now Sir Charles Dilke, who was immediately afterwards a member of the same Government as Sir William Harcourt, rakes up these expiring embers of partisan warfare, and flings about these brands after he has set them a-burning, at the very moment that he is appealing to those who love country rather than party, we must, before attempting to grapple with his words, have some little definition of their meaning. Of course, if he means to assert that any one who has the misfortune not to agree in every syllable he writes is guilty of all those wickednesses which Sir William Harcourt declared to be the peculiar attributes of the Jingo, discussion with him is closed. We naturally have no special affection, on the one hand, for the character described by Sir William Harcourt. On the other, if we have to choose between the part of pouring such language upon the heads of those who differ from us in opinion and of receiving it, we unhesitatingly prefer to be called Jingoes rather than to violate all the decencies which make fair argument possible. But apparently Sir Charles Dilke, whilst smacking his lips on almost every alternate page over the insolence which he is able subtly to convey in the use of the term "Jingo," reserving its more offensive meanings to be only understood as latent in it, usually means by it only the equivalent of chauvinism or gasconade. He expressly says so in one place; but he uses the term in so many different senses, that it is hard to know what the policy he really refers to is.

How it can be that he is "attacked by the true Jingoes for saying that we are still able to defend ourselves," we are absolutely at a loss to understand. We thought that it was the Jingoes who used to boast our ships, our men, and the like. Nay, in the very passage we quoted just now, Sir Charles Dilke spoke of the "inflated language of 1878."

It is necessary for us, therefore, to define our own position, and to explain the historical fact which, as we allege, Sir Charles Dilke has mistaken, regardless of the various meanings with which he finds it convenient to play in using this term.

Certainly, then, we at all events are not amongst those who think that our army or our fleet is at this moment so complete in its organisation that we either now have, or can be said to have had in 1878, the men and the ships that are needed for the defence of our commerce and the empire. In the main we heartily agree with very much that Sir Charles Dilke has said in these matters, though we think we shall be able to show that he has not taken the best course to remedy them.

But when Sir Charles speaks of the "inflated language of 1878," it is tolerably evident that he refers to an altogether different matter from the silly music-hall ditty which produced the name "Jingo." He manifestly refers to the tone adopted in dealing with Russia by Lord Beaconsfield and Lord Salisbury in the early months of that year. Now we assert positively what is a matter easily susceptible of historical proof, that the haughty tone then taken by our statesmen was simply founded upon absolute knowledge of the complete collapse which had attended the Russian attempt to march upon Constantinople. We do not for a moment doubt that the confession which Sir Charles Dilke now makes that his opposition to the policy of that time was not founded upon any doubt of the patriotism or the importance of the object of keeping Russia out of Constantinople, but upon a belief that we were pretending to be able to keep her out when we could not have done so, is representative not only of the opinion under which he himself acted, but that of thousands of others throughout the country at that time. Lord Randolph Churchill's Wolverhampton speech is virtually a confession that that was his view. The real facts were not known out of the Government offices. We have always held that, as a piece of party statesmanship, it was a very great mistake that steps were not taken to make them known.

We can well recall how, after the meeting of Parliament, country members came up to town saying, "Well, we have got peace certainly; but what an amount of swagger and bunkum there has been beforehand about it!"

There was no swagger and no bunkum, if by that is meant any threatening to do that which at the time we were unable to carry out. The Turkish resistance had no doubt completely collapsed. Without our action, the advance force of the Russian army could certainly have made its way into Constantinople. As certainly the force which, with the assistance of the Indian troops brought to Malta, we could have landed at Gallipoli, was enough and more than enough to have utterly defeated the feeble remnant of Russians who had passed Adrianople. It does not take a large force of well-mounted and well-trained cavalry to defeat mounted men whose horses have utterly broken down under them, and that was actually the condition of every Russian dragoon who passed the Balkans. Numerically the Russian force beyond Adrianople never exceeded 30,000 men. They were disappearing day by day, from exhaustion and illness, more rapidly than they could be replaced. Of those that did reach Adrianople, large numbers arrived by way of Varna. That supply would have been cut off the moment our fleet entered the Black Sea. If there be a fact more certain than another in history, it is that at that particular moment our position was such that, at all events till the summer, we were able by mere military and naval force alone to prohibit the advance of Russia upon Constantinople. In the then condition of the Russian army, even a Tzar could not venture to keep it till the summer, with its sea-borne supplies cut off by our fleet, and those terrible snow-covered roads, blocked with broken waggons, with dying and dead horses and men, as its sole means of being fed. Upon a knowledge of these facts alike the Tzar and the English Government acted.

But they were not understood throughout the country in England. To those who were living not immediately behind the scenes (and we ought to say, what we believe Lord Salisbury would now declare, that no Government was ever better served with information than our own was in those days), it appeared incredible that we, with all our unreadiness — with our little army and our slight preparation—could really face the power of the Tzar, whose forces even then were reputed to be counted by the million.

Englishmen revolted against what seemed to them a sham and a false pretence. They punished, as they always have punished, by their votes, a Government which acted honestly in their behalf, but acted upon information which they did not possess. There is a *naïveté* about Sir Charles Dilke's admission that he at least to this day does not know the truth, and that, had he known it, he would have been bound to appear on the opposite side to that which he took in 1880. We can afford to allow him to employ what is virtually an algebraical formula—an unknown variable—sometimes equated with Sir William Harcourt's vituperation, sometimes chauvinism, sometimes panic-mongering to his heart's content, in return for an acknowledgment at once so important and so instructive.[1]

[1] I shall have occasion in the final article to challenge the reply which Sir Charles Dilke has made to this passage, both as regards Constantinople and as regards a point not alluded to above—our power to forbid to Russia advance in Asia Minor.

I.

RUSSIA AND ENGLAND

RUSSIA AND ENGLAND.

LET us now, in regard to Russia and to England, and to the question generally of English power, draw together the points on which we desire to insist in these corrections of historical inaccuracies.

We believe, then, that twice since the establishment of the rule of force in Europe—once at the time of its inception, and once since then—it has been either the duty or the interest of England to be ready to intervene on the continent of Europe. We believe that, in either case, from the most peculiar circumstances of the time, it would have been possible for us, even as our armed forces then were, to have intervened with decisive effect; but most assuredly not in either case without a loss proportionate in men and money to the want of actual readiness for war, from which we then and now suffer. To what, then, do these experiences point? Let us consider what were in either case our points of vantage and of weakness. Beyond all doubt, our point of vantage in either case consisted in the facilities of sea transport, and in the fact that the points in which alone we were interested were easily accessible from the sea. In the case of Denmark, we believe that the fighting-power of our fleet could have been directly made to tell in aid of our land forces. In the case of the Russo-Turkish war, the enormous facilities supplied by our fleet, mercantile as well as warlike, for the transport, almost to the field of battle itself, of our whole available force, would have told with incalculable effect.

We speak grave fact, and speak in no chauvinist vein, for which, indeed, no one who really knows our actual deficiencies at this moment has any heart, when we say that no other Power in Europe could have *so quickly* subdued the Egyptian revolt as we did in 1882. The reason is simple. The force that was actually landed in Egypt, about 30,000 men, was just sufficient, not much more than sufficient, for the task assigned it; and we possessed the means—thanks to our vast mercantile marine and the efficiency of the *personnel* of our navy in such matters—of transporting at short notice that number of men, and the stores required for them on a desert march, more easily than any other European Power.

We would earnestly urge any of our readers, who suppose that these cases are altogether exceptional, to study the masterly account of the Kertch expedition, which is to be found in Mr Kinglake's eighth volume, chapter four. Every word of Mr Kinglake's wise and sound comment on the general deductions to be drawn from that experience is as worthy of examination as the striking story itself.

Compare now the case of Russia. To any point at which she desires to strike, she must, by an inexorable necessity, when we are opposed to her, convey her troops over enormous distances by land. By no manner of means, though Sir Charles Dilke and Lord Randolph Churchill exercise all the genius of man, and show a knowledge of the real conditions of warfare which, as we shall have presently occasion to show, is singularly wanting in these papers, can either of them, with the rival schemes for our military forces which they are advertising as concealed in their respective breast-pockets, enable us to compete, in point of numbers, with the paper millions of the Russian empire.

But the one advantage we do possess, that of transporting, to the very point where we want to strike, the force we can embark in England, is a power the nature of which those know best who best understand the real conditions of war. To Sir Charles Dilke it seems enough to show what forces Russia can collect at her depots. He does not understand how those terrible miles of road, over which the loyal Russian soldiery, whose heroic readiness to die, and whose patriotic and religious enthusiasm he has so truly and so well described, will stretch their limbs, present themselves to the minds of any soldier who does understand what war is. Verestchagin has, perhaps, with his terribly veracious realism, in part brought home to Londoners at least the awful truth which Sir Charles ignores. He does not see that an army wanting altogether alike in an officer and in a non-commissioned officer class, with habits of peculation engrained in those who cater for it, and suffering always from that disease of "Too much Archduke" which proved so fatal to it in 1877, enters upon any distant campaign under disadvantages which no numbers at the depots can compensate.

We cordially and heartily agree with Sir Charles Dilke that it is needful for us, for the defence of the empire, to be able to strike blows far from the shores of England. It is only an application to our time of that which, in the grandest of the Duke of Wellington's despatches, was for ever insisted on, that the true principle for an English patriot is, not to make preparation for fighting an enemy at home—though in its measure that too is needful—but to strike blows abroad which shall keep the shores of England sacred from invasion. In all reason, then, where is the weakness of our enemy at which we ought to strike? Where is the special strength which we ought to develop?

We have given illustrations which supply the answer. We were not ready, as we ought to have been, to land at once, and in effective fighting trim, upon the shores of Denmark, the force which, properly equipped and ready for war, would have pricked the bladder of the apparent strength which in February 1864 inaugurated the reign of force in Europe. We were much more ready in 1877, but we were not as ready as we ought to have been.

In each of those cases, and in 1882, exceptional opportunities—in the latter case, brilliantly seized and taken advantage of—would have enabled or did enable us to use our real power. But we cannot hope to have such opportunities in such form so presented to us as that, no matter how careless we are, we can act against armed nations, whilst we, secure in our island home, trust to the free service of our—we thank Sir Charles Dilke for so boldly asserting it—really warlike people. Not all the militia, not all the guns, not all the officers, with which he would supply us, will serve our need for the precise purpose which he has well shown that we need. Of the ultimate and essential power of England, if only time be granted her to develop it, no one, as Sir Charles Dilke himself asserts, has any doubt. What is doubtful is what she can do in the first few weeks and months of a modern war, and, as he has well shown, that is the time on which now the fatal issues hang. But no mercantile marine, not even our own, can in the first few weeks of war transport to a hostile shore AN ARMY reckoned by the hundred thousand, even if we possessed such a force. Perhaps in a month or two the transport of 200,000 ARMED MEN, if all our vast mercantile resources were strained to the utmost, and everything sacrificed to it, might be possible. But 200,000 men are not an army. If we have afoot a force of something like 70,000 men, complete in all its arms, and actually ready to take the field, that represents pretty nearly the limit of the power with which we could, under any circumstances, strike our blow. Not if we were to submit to all the strain of universal service under which the Continent is groaning; not though we spent upon our army all the milliards which Germany wrung from France, which she has employed for military service, forgotten as they have been alike by Sir Charles Dilke and Lord Randolph Churchill; not though we spent those yet vaster sums of the extraordinary budgets of France which, while they have heaped debt upon her, have created and armed her fortifications, and are quietly left out of the account of these most accurate financiers and would-be economical army reformers,—not so, or by any other means that they can devise, will England be made so ready to meet the special needs of her position, as by four simple means. First, by having her fleet actually able to perform the duties of guarding by effective offensive strokes the vast commerce—*more than double as it is of the whole carrying trade of the world outside of Greater Britain*—the guardianship of which entails upon that fleet such duties as fall to the lot of no other navies, not of all the combined navies of the world besides. Secondly, by completing the armament and garrisoning of her home fortresses and foreign coaling-stations, so that, possessed as we are of the most important points of vantage for a steam navy throughout the world, we may be able to utilise them to give power to our own fleet, instead of finding them turned to the destruction of our commerce. Thirdly, by completing, in absolute security under our own control, our telegraphic communication with our distant dependencies and outlying forts. Lastly, by having at home an effective army actually ready at any moment to be made complete; of such strength as a mercantile marine like ours can suddenly and rapidly ship, with all its stores, with all its needed land transport, and can deliver *in an unknown direction* —supported at home by such a force of volunteers and militia as will, when actual invasion threatens, in the sense in which it did in 1805, enable the whole body together to take the field, and, when it does not, will enable the active army to be employed for the defence of the empire and the fulfilment of national obligation.

Of the two rival politicians who are anxious to return to political power, by announcing that they have each discovered the philosopher's stone— Parr's Life Pills for our army and the Elixir of Life for the nation — but that the patient must be submitted to their hands before they will announce their discoveries,[1] neither of them inspires us with confidence from the circumstances under which their announcements are made. In the first place, what is it that they both declare? There is one nation in the world, and one only, which, in consequence of its political system, has hitherto submitted the management of its military and naval affairs to such as they are—to politicians bidding for place. In every other nation of the world the administration of naval and military affairs has been left to experts. The motive assigned has been a simple one. No one supposed that soldiers or sailors could not, better than poli-

[1] This is no longer fair as regards Sir Charles Dilke. He promises us at some time or other a statement of his great plan, but as yet he acts like Penelope. He will tell us his choice when he has finished spinning his large web. He is always, however, ripping what he had spun. To my thinking, no more clear and admirable account of the German army than that contained in the January 1888 'Fortnightly' has hitherto appeared in England. It is the most complete reversal of the account given in the 'Present Position of European Politics' that the most severe assailant of that volume could have published.

ticians, determine what would be most effective for war by land or sea. But—so we have been always taught—the control of the House of Commons over the *money* was necessary, to ensure that it was not misapplied or wasted. Here suddenly from the ranks of the bidders for place step out two men, who declare that the whole system has, as a matter of mere economy, utterly broken down. They both declare that those reckless countries—Germany and France—which have left the disbursement of the money and almost the determination of its amount to soldiers, and to soldiers only, have been served by them so economically that, for less money than we spend, they have secured results with which ours cannot for one moment be compared. We shall examine this question more thoroughly in our next article; but we have here to remark that, apart altogether from the palpable absurdity of comparing two countries which take their men by compulsion, with a country which pays in the dearest market in the world at the market rate, these gentlemen have, as we hinted above, directly miscalculated the expenditure of France and Germany by millions. Lord Randolph Churchill has certainly done it more recklessly and openly than Sir Charles Dilke. There is just the difference between them of a *suggestio falsi* as against a *suppressio veri*. Lord Randolph, though in another part of his speech he shows that he knows what huge sums France has borrowed of late years, yet tells the men of Wolverhampton that, in comparing the *ordinary* expenditure of France and England, the complete armament of the German and French fortresses is to be compared with the deficiencies of ours.[1] Does he or does he not know how much of that huge debt, which has rolled up since the war of 1870, has been expended on placing the fortifications and armament of France on a proper footing? Furthermore, we charge both of them with having absolutely ignored the extent and nature of the work which our fleet has to do; and we refuse to place confidence in financiers who begin by showing that they cannot make estimates of expenditure without errors in the millions, while they at the same time show that they do not understand in the least what the nature of the task they have to undertake is.

There are grave deficiencies in the condition of our defences both at home and in our distant fortresses. We certainly have no wish to underrate them, or to deny that many of those defects which Lord Randolph has described really exist. But why is it that both these gentlemen select the present moment to bring before the public these defects of our condition? From whom was it that

[1] 'Times' report, June 4, 1887, of speech at Wolverhampton.

Lord Randolph Churchill learnt all those weaknesses of our condition which need to be remedied? The answer is simple enough. It is because for the first time a Cabinet has courageously faced them. Because his colleagues laid before him these necessities of our condition, and proposed to remedy them. Above all, because one quiet, business-like, silent man, the present leader of the House of Commons, has insisted in office and out of office upon the all-importance of actually and effectively placing our coaling-stations in a condition which will enable our fleet to rely upon them, instead of having to defend them. As General Brackenbury explained, in behalf of the Secretary of State, to the United Service Institution, more effective steps have been taken within the time of Mr Smith's tenure of the War Office than during any preceding period, to arrange, as far as can be done on our present expenditure, for carrying out those reforms which we have laid down as essential for developing to the full our real power. They are steps only: but steps have been taken towards providing that we shall have garrisons available for our home fortresses, and for our coaling-stations, and above all, for making it possible for us to strike for the defence of the empire, by having ready *as an army* two corps and an effective cavalry division available to go anywhere and do anything.[1] That scheme has not been fully carried out, and cannot be fully carried out till all parties in the state are agreed as to what is necessary. Why has it not gone further as yet? Sir Charles Dilke has supplied the answer—"The recent fit of economy promoted by Lord Randolph Churchill." That has not, indeed, acted in the way he has assumed. It has not induced the Cabinet to make *reductions* on their estimates. We must confess that a Cabinet placed in so critical a position as the present one was at the moment of Lord Randolph's escapade, seems to us to have displayed a patriotic courage rare in our times, and to deserve from a Radical who is specially anxious to appeal to those who cast aside personal and partisan feeling, somewhat better treatment than Sir Charles Dilke gives them in his mode of dealing with Lord Randolph's boasted economy. Otherwise we have nothing to object to in the following argument: "With a still weaker Government, a Chancellor of the Exchequer of equal boldness might on this principle claim credit for saving the whole amount of the army and navy expenditure of the country. He would indeed possibly be borne in triumph for it, although also possibly afterwards hanged when the country found that he had been wrong in his calcu-

---

[1] See General Brackenbury's speech at United Service Institution, separately issued.

lations" (p. 295). Neither have we any objection to the statement, that some of the revelations recently made would "justify the hanging of a few ex-Secretaries of State for War" (p. 314).

But, in fact, the unfortunate effect of Lord Randolph's action has been this: instead of boldly asking for all that was required to make our two corps and our cavalry division actually available for fighting in England, or for transfer abroad, and for furnishing the garrison artillerymen, who are sorely needed to make our fortresses of any use, the order has gone forth that, at present at all events, only so much should be done as could be managed by robbing Peter to pay Paul. The absolute necessity, if our troops are to be able to fight at all, of having ammunition columns for such artillery and infantry as we do send into the field, has unfortunately, owing to the fact that the estimates could not be increased, led to a reduction in the artillery. The particular necessities which it is now proposed to provide are precisely those, many of them named by Sir Charles Dilke, which are required to enable us to take advantage of our volunteers and militia in making secure our fortresses, in providing generally for their co-operation with an effective army in the field, and for enabling such an army as we could at once transport from England to act immediately on being landed.

Much undoubtedly remains to be done, but, for

our own part, we heartily echo the words in which the Earl of Wemyss, for years the most energetic protestant against the neglect of those very measures which are at least now officially proposed, declared General Brackenbury's speech to be the most important, and, on the whole, *comforting* statement that has been made in our time. Money has undoubtedly been wasted in the past. Sir James Fitz-James Stephen's Commission has shown how and why it has been wasted. Unfortunately, a perusal of that report does not tend to confirm Lord Randolph's allegation that the condition of the House of Commons, the strife of parties, and the supremacy of talkers, or of men who are political partisans first and administrators afterwards, has not been the chief cause of the evil.

But the moment when, in a quiet business-like way and for the first time, the real difficulties have at least been fairly acknowledged, is not the one for throwing in the face of the present men the crimes of their predecessors. We heartily wish to see the whole question referred to that authoritative body, independent of party, for which Sir Charles Dilke and Lord Wolseley alike ask. Such a body must first determine the true meaning of the preamble of the Army Act—that is, how "the possessions of her Majesty's crown" are to be defended. We believe that they would find that the very small reduction in the total force of our field-guns, horse-artillery and field-artillery together, is not, as Sir Charles Dilke has averred, dangerous as a symptom, but that it is a part, however unfortunate a part, of a response to the earnest instances of those who have been for years pressing for genuine efficiency. But we are bound to admit that when we talk of genuine efficiency, we cannot accept Sir Charles Dilke's mode of determining what efficiency is.

It happens that the particular occasion on which General Brackenbury's speech was delivered will enable us to show one instance—we shall take another as conclusive before we have done—of the degree to which Sir Charles Dilke is to be depended on as a military authority, or rather as capable by his *ipse dixit* of erecting into decisive military authorities certain people carefully kept behind the veil, to whom he constantly refers as *the* exponents of true military wisdom.

"The volunteers," says Sir Charles, "however useful they may be as garrison artillery, will never be able in large numbers to manage field-artillery" (p. 315). And again: "Sir Edward Hamley, indeed, has suggested that it is a positive advantage to this country, that while the force which will attack us will, by the nature of things, be provided only with field-artillery, our defending force will be supplied with guns of position—that is, with guns of heavier weight; as though a small trained army, making a dash on London, would be likely to advance directly upon intrenched positions, armed with heavy guns, when it could so easily march into London by twenty other different routes" (p. 315).

We should have thought that a soldier who has devoted his life to the subject of strategy, the author of the greatest book on that matter in the English language, speaking about his own arm of the service, might have been treated with a little more respect than this. Sir Charles Dilke evidently does not know his man. He is himself a clever writer and a clever politician. But cleverer writers, some of the greatest whom our times have seen, have before now cowered before the lash he has provoked. Abler politicians than he have winced when Sir Edward's pen has been employed to expose sentences not quite so silly as this.

Sir Charles talks about Jomini, but he evidently has never heard that, though big guns are ugly customers, there are such things as what are known to soldiers as "attractive positions," in which big guns call a hostile army towards them with more subtly winning voice than any siren singing from her rocks. The Russian army found that out when, willy-nilly, Plevna had to be tackled.

Most assuredly, "guns of position" will not supply the place of highly mobile field-artillery, but yet there are few armies that would not rejoice in their aid if they could procure them in such numbers as we can obtain for English service by the aid of the volunteers. Not rarely their effect would be decisive.

As we have hinted, the discussion at the United Service Institution, at which General Brackenbury was authorised to explain the scheme which Mr W. H. Smith had approved and Mr Stanhope has accepted from him, was devoted to the discussion of this very subject of volunteer field-artillery.

General Brackenbury, himself one of the most distinguished of living English artillery officers, pointed out the absence of any artillery to support our militia and volunteer infantry. Sir Charles Dilke has mentioned it in these words: "This country, in the event of invasion, would put some 300,000 militia and volunteer infantry in line; and in order to feel secure with such a force, we ought, according to the ordinary rules of war, to have 900 properly worked guns at home."[1]

General Brackenbury, it is true, did not talk about "the ordinary rules of war." It is an expression which trained soldiers are rather apt to avoid, because war knows few "rules," though many principles; and further, both alike are apt to vary in their application, according to circumstances and the nature of the country in which war is carried on. Again, few soldiers who have ever

[1] Present Position of European Politics, p. 314.

carefully and practically considered the question of the defence of England can fail to be aware that the nature of the country restricts and modifies the ordinary use of artillery in a very marked degree. Further, as large numbers of the volunteers would be required for garrison work, he puts our active field-army for home defence at 130,000 infantry, besides the two corps and cavalry division, so that the deficiency in field-guns would be 390—not 900. But he asked whether any possible augmentation of so expensive an arm as the royal artillery or royal horse-artillery, that the country could be expected to grant, would supply this deficiency. We confess to some curiosity for a sight of that most economical budget of Sir Charles Dilke's, which, in addition to supplying all that we at present have and an army of Continental size ready to be transported by sea at a moment's notice, is to furnish us with an augmentation of 900 royal artillery field-guns. These will, of course, consist chiefly of horse-artillery on Sir Charles's principles.[1]

[1] Sir Charles has complained that I have here too closely tied him to the figure of "900." I have simply followed the only clue he had given to the numbers he proposed to supply. I certainly shall be delighted to get the additional security provided by 390 royal artillery guns, *if the country will pay for them ! ! !* But before the end of this volume I think I shall be able to show that the expenditure ought not to be incurred till we are sure that our fleet is all that it ought to be, and till our harbours and coaling-stations are secure, hardly even till our world-telegraph system is complete. Certainly the thing cannot be done on the principle

But meantime, till we are furnished either by Sir Charles Dilke or Lord Randolph with the rival philosophers' stones which are thus to coin gold for us, we are content to accept the authority of Sir E. Hamley and General Brackenbury. At this meeting other very able artillery officers confessed that, having had to overcome great prejudices in that matter, they had, from actual trial and experience of the working of volunteer field-artillery, come to the conviction that it could be made most efficient. We believe, then, that the decision of the Government is a sound one, that they will reverse the policy of their predecessors and do their utmost to encourage the development of volunteer heavy field-artillery. We should have thought that a man so anxious as Sir Charles Dilke to appeal to those who cast aside "personal" —we presume, therefore, professional—prejudice, might have guessed who are likely to be giving at this moment the best advice,—three such artillery officers as Sir Edward Hamley, General Brackenbury, and Colonel Shakespeare; or those who think that there is nothing like leather, and that volunteers must be warned off the sacred field of the royal artillery.

Before leaving this question of the artillery, we

assumed by Sir Charles Dilke, when he wrote 'The Present Position of European Politics,' "that it is not in expenditure that we fall short" (p. 287).

may as well note the recklessness with which, so far as English officers are concerned, Sir Charles Dilke goes out of his way to enlist against him those whom most Englishmen look upon as of some weight, as English soldiers go, in matters of practical war. Again and again he alleges that Lord Wolseley was positively in favour of the reduction of the horse-artillery *per se*, speaking of it as the "theatrical" element in war. Now, a reference to Lord Wolseley's speech shows that in it the horse-artillery was not mentioned. It was a purely gratuitous assumption that in speaking of the "theatrical" element he referred to the recent reduction of that arm. We have reason to know that, in Sir Charles Dilke's behalf, Lord Wolseley's attention was called to Sir Charles's statement, and that he replied, not only that he had not said anything whatever of the kind, but that he was thinking of altogether other matters; and that he added,—" No one regrets more than I do the reduction of the horse-artillery; but as we had to choose between keeping guns we could not use, and supplying, by their disestablishment, what was indispensable to make the army we can use as a whole effective, we had very reluctantly to dispense with them."

Sir Charles's attention was drawn to the substance of these statements prior to the publication of the recent article; yet he retained the words in inverted commas, as though Lord Wolseley had actually spoken of the "theatrical horse-artillery."[1]

Sir Charles has endeavoured to pour cold water on the efforts at present being made to produce an effective force of two army-corps and a cavalry division, by referring constantly to what, quoting Mr Stanhope, he calls the "abortive scheme of eight army-corps." We confess that we regret the phrase. The author of that scheme, now dead many years, was a soldier of first-rate ability, who did very great service to the English army, and we have a dislike to the process of kicking dead lions. But the scheme, such as it was, was never intended to do more than expose the weaknesses of our condition. When Sir Charles says that "the defence made for the reduction of the horse-artillery has revealed that, for all practical purposes, we may be said to have no artillery for the volunteer and militia infantry," it is clear that he has never looked at that scheme. Each "army-corps" was shown as it would be for peace service, with blanks at every point where deficiencies existed. If members of Parliament like Sir Charles Dilke neglected to look at it, and therefore did not take the hint or ask any questions about it,

---

[1] As Sir Charles Dilke has in his recent articles quoted words which show that Lord Wolseley in the abstract wishes for an increase, not a reduction, of the artillery, I have here suppressed a long extract from a speech which was given to prove that point.

what becomes of Lord Randolph's contention, that the House of Commons is nowise to blame for our present condition?

The work, of which Mr Hardy spoke, on railways and the like, was actually done; and though changes in the units of the army involve some corrections in it now, the substance of it remains available, and is habitually used by all staff officers, trained during the last ten years, in the consideration of railway schemes and such matters. What is now being done is of an altogether different kind, and no one would have more rejoiced to see it worked out than the author of that old scheme, though he would be perhaps amused to find that shafts aimed at his "abortive" effort have tended to rebound against the very different and most important scheme of to-day, to which he would have looked forward as to a promised land he was not permitted to see.

So far, then, as our own immediate offensive strength against Russia is concerned, we hold that it depends first on our navy; and secondly, upon our being able to prepare for instant action as large a force as we can promptly ship from our ports. We ought at least, in the first instance, to work up to the standard at which the Government is now aiming: that of putting two army-corps and a cavalry division into a condition for effective action abroad, the only true and proper defence of our empire. We believe firmly that no German military authority would look upon the power we should so possess as the equivalent only of the force of Roumania. The Roumanian army in the field may be considerably larger than two *corps d'armée* and a cavalry division. It is one thing to have such a force on land; it is another thing to be able to deliver with it a blow in any direction we choose, while we also possess the command of the sea. It is almost certain that we shall never have to enter into any quarrel in which we cannot on the *do ut des* principle obtain allies. In any alliance, the command of the sea, such a force so capable of movement, and the financial support of England, will be of priceless value. If Germany, as Sir Charles Dilke alleges, in the beginning of of 1887 advised Austria to reject our alliance, we think we can tell him the reason. In 1882 Germany took the greatest pains to ascertain precisely what power we had shown in Egypt. A very short inquiry enabled Major von Hagenau, the Commissioner with our army, to ascertain that the force which captured Cairo was not, in the European sense, a mobile army at all, and that, but for the seizure of the railway and canal, transport would for it have been an insuperable difficulty. If Major von Hagenau had been able to record the fact that, apart from the force which we brought from India, which was in all respects fit to take the field, we had had a really mobile army of two *corps d'armée* and a cavalry division capable of being transported at a moment's notice anywhere, his view of the question would have been a very different one.

But in order that such a force, able to serve as a nucleus for auxiliaries, may also be able to strike effectively, it is essential to us that entry should be possible for us into the Black Sea, as well as into the Baltic. We shall endeavour in our final article [1] to show that the nature of the alliances which it is to our advantage to form is of such a kind that if we do not restrict ourselves to the defence of India, but meet Russian aggression where other Powers have an interest in resisting it, we place ourselves on a footing of vantage which we almost absolutely lose if we restrict ourselves to the defence of India. In India itself our whole advantage lies in forcing Russia to act as far from her base as possible, and in striking her line of communications through Persia, as has been admirably pointed out by Colonel Malleson.[2] To announce beforehand that we restrict aggression to an attack upon Vladivostock, is to abandon the most effective part of our special strength—the uncertainty of the direction of our blow.

---

[1] See IV., " Italy, Turkey, and English Alliances."
[2] See Colonel Malleson's article, 'Blackwood's Magazine,' April 1887, " The Fortnightly Reviewer and Russia."

It is rather remarkable that in speaking of Vladivostock Sir Charles Dilke has not drawn attention to the essentially *offensive* purpose with which Russia is strengthening her fleet at that point. Yet it is no secret that had war with Russia broken out a few years ago, it was her purpose to have struck thence directly upon our Australian colonies, and that the knowledge of that fact has been the great motive which has led our colonists to set seriously to work to arm and prepare themselves. It may, no doubt, on that account be necessary that one of our earliest blows should be struck at Vladivostock.

We by no means desire to underrate the danger of Russian power, and of the steady purpose with which she pursues her aims against us. The danger with which Russia menaces us is her steady progress towards our Indian frontier, extending her dominion over tribes at such a distance from us that we cannot with advantage to ourselves reach her during her progress; while yet she is continually more and more able to employ those tribes in harassing us. She can so, almost without effort, entail costly expenditure upon us. Therefore it appears to be our true policy to forbid her advance, and to enforce that prohibition by attacking her where we can get at her. We can only do this by European action, to which we contribute our legitimate share. Hence it becomes of the greatest importance to judge what the real character of the Russian army is, and whether it is, as Sir Charles Dilke has alleged, so overwhelmingly powerful in Europe that, even with such allies as will be glad to join us in the task of opposing it, we have reason to fear the issue.

The Russian infantry undoubtedly has those characteristics of which Sir Charles Dilke has spoken. The men are ready to die silently and without troublesome inquiries as to what they are ordered to do. As long as it was possible to form masses of them into great columns, and to push them forward, regardless of loss of life, into the field of battle, the power of their obstinate heroism and of their numbers was enormous. But the effects of the breech-loader on the character of modern fighting had been felt by all Europe eleven long years before the Turkish war. Russian officers had realised them as fully as others; and it was only the impossibility of handling the men under the fixed conditions of modern war, that obliged them to sacrifice life with such melancholy results as attended the attempt of 1877-78 upon Constantinople. The national characteristics of the Russian peasantry have not changed. The conditions of Russian life, and the absence of the men who could intelligently lead them in the subordinate ranks, is a fact as marked as ever. All military observers who look below the surface note it now as much as then. These factors in the estimate are ignored by Sir Charles Dilke.[1]

Strangely enough, he seems, in relation to the cavalry, to have awakened to the fact that we are in a period of war when the breech-loader counts for something. He is so affected by it, that he propounds a theory that cavalry can now only act in war, without being destroyed, by adopting the method which the Tzar has chosen for his Cossacks. The Russian cavalry of all classes have recently been converted into a sort of imitation of the mounted rifles who constituted the cavalry of the American war. The Cossacks are not trained infantry soldiers, in any sense of the term. They are not men accustomed from childhood to the use of rifles, as were the American marksmen. They are as unlike highly effective mounted infantry as it is possible for men to be. Yet Sir Charles would impress on his readers the belief that there is no kind of doubt as to their superiority to all cavalry

---

[1] Sir Charles Dilke, who treats Inkermann as ancient history, has in his January 1888 article appealed to the fact that "against Russian troops the veterans of Frederick the Great and of Napoleon struggled *in vain*." The French, it is needless to say, cherish a curious delusion about the "sun of Austerlitz" and a few other matters, such as the causes which led to the capture of Moscow and the retreat from it. But apart from that, I would earnestly press that Mr Kinglake's account of Inkermann should be actually studied. It will there be seen that the Russians then attempted to employ modern Prussian tactics and failed because of national characteristics just as they did in 1877.

which trusts chiefly to the proper weapon of the true cavalry soldier—the *arme blanche*. There is no country in Europe from which decisive authority may not be quoted against him on the other side.

In the year 1882, Von Moltke's opinion, and that of the German military leaders generally, was decisively expressed on the subject, in consequence of the publication of a book declaring that the day of cavalry was over, and that the sooner armies got rid of "this lumber" the better. Von Moltke in that year, in a letter which may be read in the 'Revue Militaire de l'Étranger,' pronounced a strong opinion that only the want of more perfect handling prevented the German cavalry, during the 1870 campaign, from producing even greater results on the field of battle than they actually did, great as those results were. The Germans continually, at their manœuvres, practise their cavalry in surprise charges with the *arme blanche*.

As to Austrian opinion, no military reader in any nation of Europe shares that profound contempt for the Archduke Albrecht which is expressed by Sir Charles Dilke, when he says that the Austrians have now no great leaders. Most soldiers look upon Albrecht as a very skilful leader indeed, and would trust his opinion on a point of this kind rather than that of almost any man in Europe. Now it happens that quite recently the Archduke has expressed his conviction that the change which has been made in the Russian cavalry has ruined its efficiency. The Austrian cavalry leaders—and they are among the best in Europe—all take that view, and would like few things so well as to lead their men against those motley riding footmen, who are neither, in any shape, fish, flesh, nor good redherring.

French opinion, whether as expressed in the masterly papers which have appeared in their "conferences," in the 'Revue Militaire,' and in the 'Journal des Sciences Militaires,' or as shown by their actual cavalry training, is on the same side.

But the most effective exposure of all of the weaknesses of the present Russian cavalry has come from a Russian pen. Few sounder or more able papers on the modern service of cavalry have ever been written than that by Colonel Baïkov, which has been rendered available for general reading by an excellent translation in a recent number of the 'Revue Militaire de l'Étranger.'[1]

Colonel Baïkov shows that not only is the present system contrary to all sound principle, but that it is hopelessly unsuited to the habits and traditions of the Russian cavalry itself. Further, he takes the history of the use of the Russian cavalry during the 1877 - 1878 campaign, and declares that they were then employed chiefly

[1] Revue Militaire de l'Étranger, vol. xxx. pp. 139-149 (issue of 15th Aug. 1886).

in service on foot; so used, he declares, that *they were not able even to stop convoys.* He declares that they expended, without producing an effect, a million and a quarter of cartridges.

On one notable occasion a picked body of them, selected expressly because of their supposed shooting quality, were despatched with orders to stop a particular convoy in the neighbourhood of Plevna. Having reached a point as near as it was thought desirable for them to move as a mounted corps, they left their horses behind them and advanced to attack, only to be driven off by a small party of Turkish soldiery, without doing the latter any damage whatever. Colonel Baïkov shows further that all the recent changes have tended to aggravate these defects.

Yet this is the cavalry of which Sir Charles Dilke tells us that it is the only mounted force in Europe adapted to the modern conditions of war!

It is on data like these that he determines the power in Europe of the Russian army and its relative condition as compared with the armies of Austria and Germany.[1]

---

[1] In his last article Sir Charles Dilke throws out a remark which touches me nearly. He says, "It ill becomes the advocates of mounted infantry to speak lightly" of the new Russian cavalry. Now I have been for at least sixteen years the enthusiastic advocate of the use of "mounted infantry." Having during that time seen again and again the services which our own mounted infantry has

So sure is he of his facts, that he is convinced that this cavalry force alone will sweep away the feeble resistance of the Austrians, and render their mobilisation impossible. So overwhelming is the force of Russia, that it is useless for us to attempt to rely upon such feeble reeds as any of the other Continental armies; and therefore, such is the logical conclusion, we had better fight this gigantic Power alone on our own resources, and having warned her where we intend to attack her, prepare at home our future expedition against Vladivostock by a system almost entirely dependent on a developed militia.[1]

We certainly do not deny the numerical force of the Russian artillery. But artillery is an arm exceptionally difficult to send in vast masses great distances from home, over difficult country; and it is still more difficult under such conditions to keep it supplied with the forage and the ammunition it needs. If our points of attack are well chosen, however great may be the numbers of the Russian artillery at home, we ought not on the field of

rendered us in our own expeditions, I have no kind of doubt of the services they would render us in European warfare. It is because I do not think that the Russian dismounted Cossacks fulfil the conditions required of good mounted infantry that I disbelieve in them. Cavalry and mounted infantry are each invaluable arms, but you cannot mash them together without destroying them for their proper work.

[1] This, the scheme apparently suggested in the "Position of European Politics," has been abandoned in the more recent articles.

battle to meet with them in overwhelming force. They certainly in 1877 did not do much to prepare the way for the assaults of their infantry.

We do not propose to follow Sir Charles Dilke into a numerical comparison between the depot forces of Russia and our own. For the reasons we have alleged, the comparison appears to us to be absolutely futile. It is, as Bismarck long since said, a question, when the comparison is so made, of a contest between an elephant and a whale. There is, however, one element in our strength which neither we nor Russia can safely ignore. Sir Lepel Griffin has lately spoken, with an authority almost beyond dispute, of the zeal with which the feudatory princes of India would aid us to resist a transfer of authority in the East from us to Russia. That is a point on which we cannot now dwell at length, but it is an element in the question not to be ignored.

To sum up, then, the conclusions towards which we desire to lead. We shall find, when we come to examine the conditions under which foreign nations maintain their huge armies, that, though our own army in proportion to numbers costs sums which *appear* to be fabulously large in proportion to theirs, yet that in mere monetary resources the drain of their system is incalculably greater than ours. Our own army is, as we believe, the cheapest in the world for the work it has to do. Though much money has been wasted in the past, and though many reforms are needed, we are now, in the main, upon the right track, provided the public will so far interest itself in the matter as to see that abuses, which have crept in, mainly because of that very parliamentary system which Lord Randolph acquits, are remedied. The navy is now in hands which earnestly intend to sift its weaknesses and redress what is wrong;[1] but it has a gigantic task in defending a commerce, the extent and the weakness of which, before attack, is never realised by Englishmen. On the other hand, that commerce supplies to us a special power for striking effective blows at a distance from home, which of its kind is unrivalled.

We are beyond question in the main, as both Sir Charles Dilke and Colonel Malleson are agreed, within India itself restricted to an essentially defensive position. Any contest with Russia in which Russia should be able to strike, and we only to defend, would be a disastrous one. Therefore we need to develop our power for striking rapidly as far as we reasonably may. The inexorable conditions of sea transport impose a limit which cannot be passed to the force that can so be used for striking rapidly.

If we believed—which we do not—that Vladivostock was the one vulnerable point in the Russian

[1] Written whilst Lord Charles Beresford was at the Admiralty.

dominions at which we could strike, we should hold Sir Charles Dilke to be a traitor for disclosing our purpose of going there, seeing that all effective strokes depend on their being delivered after the fashion of our movement in 1882 from Alexandria to Ismailia, of which Arabi never heard till he was a prisoner in Ceylon.[1] Therefore we do not propose to discuss the exact direction in which our blow should be delivered, but in our final article we shall show cause why the power of entering the Black Sea is vitally important to us.

The efforts which are being made at the present moment by the Government to put matters on a right footing, and to face facts, deserve the support of every patriotic Englishman. They only need to be supported against the purveyors of nostrums on the right hand and on the left, and to be encouraged to ask for what they ought to have, concealing nothing.

Lastly, we propose to show that the present condition of the Continent offers us the opportunity, on the *do ut des* principle, of alliance, which is vital to us if we are to defend our empire without ruinous strain on our people.

---

[1] Here, as in several instances where the case of the Egyptian campaign of 1882 is mentioned, I may now refer to the official history of that war, which has been published since the articles were written.

II.

GERMANY, FRANCE, AND BELGIUM

GERMANY, FRANCE, AND BELGIUM.

WE propose now to take in order the following questions, which were raised in our last article under the general heading :—

I. We intend, by comparing the methods which are employed by Germany for raising her forces with our own methods, to maintain our thesis—that our own army is the cheapest in the world, in proportion to the work it has to do. It will be seen that our contention is that our army payments represent a money sacrifice to the country so incomparably less than the monetary sacrifice which her methods oblige Germany to make, that no subsequent care and economy on the part of German officials in the expenditure of cash, when it has once been obtained, can prevent ours from being, as a question of money, the more economical method of the two. We wish clearly at the outset to separate this question from that of the expenditure of the money, in which we have everything to learn from Germany, and Germany has little or nothing to learn from us. We shall therefore, in the first instance, deal with Lord Randolph's notions of economy, and show that neither English nor German experience supports them. We shall then endeavour to make good our case as to the enormous sacrifices which Germany is making as compared with ourselves. We shall be content to establish this in the case of Germany alone, because the whole administration of Germany is in its expenditure so notoriously wise and economical, that, if Germany cannot make a compulsory service and a state manipulation of huge funds of money economical, it is certain that no other Power can do so.

II. We propose next to discuss the relative strength of the present French and German military frontiers—as to which we directly challenged Sir Charles Dilke's statement that the French frontier is now the stronger of the two. It will be seen, when we come to describe the two frontiers, that there are most plausible grounds for Sir Charles Dilke's belief; that it is well that the question should have been raised; that the views and principles which induce the German strategists to prefer a method of defence altogether different from that of France, do not lie on the surface.

Nevertheless we believe that we shall be able to show that they are sound and true. In any case, the views of the two great military Powers are so startlingly different, that we think a statement of them, intelligible to non-military readers, cannot fail to be of interest. It will prepare such readers, at least, to study the events which will occur on the outbreak of war whenever it takes place.

III. The third point in relation to France and Germany, on which we challenged Sir Charles's statements, is this. He assumes that, as a necessary consequence of the enormous strength of the new French frontier, Germany will certainly be disposed to march through Belgium. We propose to show that there are strong military reasons, involved in the nature of the case, which tend to turn the balance the other way. At the same time, we must at once admit that, though we differ from Sir Charles as to the extent to which the military balance tends to sway in this direction, we do not differ from him in thinking that if Belgium would ensure her liberties she must effectually arm.

IV. Connected with this is the next question, which immediately concerns ourselves, whether we have abandoned all purpose of fulfilling the international obligations we have undertaken, provided that Belgium performs her part. On this matter we protested that Sir Charles Dilke had no adequate grounds for the conclusion he had arrived at. We intend therefore to show, in the first place, to what extent it is probable that we should be able to make good our support of Belgian neutrality in the event of a war between France and Germany. In the second, we shall quote the words of our statesmen, at the time when the question last arose, to show how clear and certain our responsibility is. We shall declare our disbelief that Englishmen intend to abandon an acknowledged duty.

V. We shall next discuss in general terms the present efficiency of the two opposing armies. It seems to us essential to enter, so far as we may, into these matters, if the mere numerical figures which Sir Charles Dilke has supplied are to have any practical value.

This will occupy all the space we can afford for the present. In our third article we shall first discuss, in a similar manner, the frontiers opposed to one another of Russia and Germany, and the relative advantages for offence and defence presented by them to each Power; secondly, the position of Germany, in alliance with Austria, in a war against Russia and France, and the general character of Austria as a military Power; thirdly, we shall have to reply to the statements made in Sir Charles Dilke's now published volume on that matter, which is for us always the central "couple," as the mathematicians would call it, of the European balance—Russia and England—in relation to European war. In every instance this is the point towards which we desire to lead up; but we shall not be able to complete our statement in regard to it until our final article, after we have completed our survey of the other Powers involved in the present conditions of most unstable equilibrium.

I. *German and English Economy.*—Economy, says Lord Randolph Churchill, and efficiency go hand in hand. We agree with him. We believe that efficiency is always economical, provided you can afford to pay for it. That is the secret of the true German economy. Lord Randolph has well illustrated the meaning which he attaches to the phrase by the questions which he put to witnesses in the Parliamentary Committee of which he is chairman. He did not leave much doubt of his meaning in the Wolverhampton speech. Let us illustrate Lord Randolph's philosophy, and show its universal soundness and applicability to the current experience of English life: "Pay for shoddy, and you are sure to get good English broadcloth. Pay for butterine, and you are sure to get the best Dorsetshire butter. Pay for cheap clothes, and you are sure not to get nasty. Mark your lawyer's brief with the lowest of known fees; you are sure to secure the services of the most leading counsel and their constant attendance on your suit. Seek out where you can consult a physician for a ten-shilling fee, and you are sure to get the advice of the best specialists in London." Such is Lord Randolph's knowledge of the world. Is it really possible that, apart from all German experience, of which he manifestly knows nothing, Lord Randolph never read the masterly essay on Lord Clive, which describes how that Indian administration was created, the efficiency of which has been the standing admiration of all foreign critics? Lord Randolph should, at least, know something of India.

"Clive saw clearly that it was absurd to give men power and to require them to live in penury. He justly concluded that no reform could be effectual which should not be coupled with a plan for liberally remunerating the civil servants of the Company." That is Lord Macaulay's account of economical administration. Again, if Lord Randolph chooses to call before his Committee those who know the present administration of the War Office, we venture to predict this: that he will find there is one conviction shared by them all, be they who they may—soldier, clerk, those who wish to see a stronger military element infused into the department, those who wish for some other reforms, and those who wish to keep things as they are,—all, we say, have alike one conviction on one subject connected with that Office. It is this: that the cheapest service for which the country has at this moment to pay, done by any of the civil staff, is that of the most highly paid permanent civil servant within it. Many private jealousies and personal piques are engendered by sedentary work; yet within the walls of the War Office, and among those who have business relations with it, all will agree that every pound of money that is paid for Sir Ralph Thompson's salary is more economically expended than most other two pounds that go out of her Majesty's Exchequer.

We say, then, that on English evidence alone Lord Randolph's notions of economy by cheeseparing cutting down of salaries is a false one. We say further, that if, ignoring our own experience, the experience of America, and the experience of Germany, with which we are now about to deal, he appeals simply to the prejudices which induce working men to believe that any one who gets higher pay than they do must be overpaid, he will be the deadliest enemy that his country has had to encounter for years. He will bring about a costly collapse of our administration as well as of our army, such as it would not be possible for any one, who has not an influence over the democracy so powerful for good and evil as his own, to cause.

As a question of the factors that must go to determine the propriety of the salaries paid in Germany and England, we ask our readers to consider this report of an actual conversation which took place a year or two ago in German society, not certainly in Berlin, but as it happens in Dresden. We change only the names.

"What extraordinarily lucky people those Von Cobos are!"

"Why, what has happened?"

"Haven't you heard?"

"No; tell me."

"Why, Fräulein von Cobo is engaged to be married to a man with £300 a-year!"

Literally that took place, and represented the general feeling of society: £300 a-year—all told —was looked upon as an independent fortune on which a "Von" was to be congratulated as a quite exceptional piece of luck.

How can you compare, by merely citing figures, salaries under such circumstances in London and in Dresden or in most parts of Germany? It does not matter a bit whether the difference results from a more economical style of living or from money actually purchasing more. The man in office has to live in England as it is.

Let us take another illustration to make this point clear. A few years ago it was necessary to send a distinguished English officer to command the native Egyptian army. He found that, tempting to an able soldier as that position was, he would have been obliged to refuse it unless there had been attached to it an income of several thousands a-year. For, living in the society of the Pashas of Cairo, a grandee among them, he must either have beggared his own family or have put himself in a false position if he had not received an adequate salary.

Lord Randolph says that the point of a Secretary of State in England receiving about double the pay of a similar official in Berlin is irrelevant. It may be convenient to him for his own purposes to allege that that is so, but he either ignores or forgets an important historical discussion. When last the salaries of our great State officials were publicly attacked, the strongest and most convincing argument by which they were defended was this from the then Lord John Russell: "I have been a poor man all my life, but I never knew what it was to be in debt till I became a Secretary of State."

Thus it is especially on poor men that the strain falls of positions of power to which no adequate salary is attached; the State instantly suffers, since the choice necessarily falls on men of inferior capacity and character, who are rich enough to take the office. That is the most foolish of all unwise economies.

In Prussia there is not a rich class, independent of its pay, from which fairly efficient officers might be drawn. So thoroughly is the necessity of paying for efficient services, if you desire economy, understood in Germany, that a few years ago a somewhat startling surprise disturbed an arrangement of Mr Gladstone's. Thinking that the economical conditions of Prussia must involve lower rates of pay for her officers, which would enable him to propose curtailment of expense in the pay of the English army, he called for a return of the pay of all ranks of the officers of the German army. The return brought out facts so little to Mr Gladstone's taste, that the document was never presented to the House of Commons, for whom it was originally intended.

General Brackenbury, in his evidence before Lord Randolph's Committee, has given such full particulars on this subject that we need not enlarge on them here. He has shown that, while the junior officers of the German army receive, in comparison with the conditions of civil life and with civil salaries, very much higher pay than our own, some of our higher grades receive much larger pay than the German. But we could easily prove that Lord Russell's speech applies strictly to these cases. As an instance, the expenses of the Portsmouth command are so great that it is impossible to appoint any officer to it who has not a private income of *several* thousands a-year. A distinguished cavalry officer, who has no children, and is certainly not a poor man, told the present writer that, much as he should like to accept the command of the cavalry at Aldershot, he feared he should not be able to afford to do so. The nominal pay of a full "general" in England only obtains for a man in actual command in the field. In that position he is a much poorer man than the German "general" with half his salary. The English general has necessarily to incur the expenses of the political hospitalities of England. He has to entertain princes. All such expenses fall on the German Emperor. High as is the nominal pay of an English Commander-in-Chief in the field, the command in most of our recent expeditions has been in each instance almost pecuniarily ruinous to the actual leader. We challenge Lord Randolph to investigate the exact accuracy of every one of these statements. If he really desires the good of his country, he can hardly refuse to test them when thus laid before him. If not, perhaps some other member of the Committee will keep the matter in mind.

We may take, as an illustration of the German views of wise expenditure, the fact that when, during the Revolutionary period of 1848, the Prussian Reds broke into the Government arsenal, they found there a complete store of *rifled* small-arms, ready for issue to the whole army, at a time when none of the wealthy Powers of Europe, not even England, had ventured to incur the outlay of purchasing rifles for the rank and file. Again, in 1864, Prussia had completely re-armed her soldiers with breech-loaders before any of the wealthier Powers had done so. For the third time now she has just completed, or is just completing, the issue to all her troops of magazine rifled small-arms. For the third time, in this expenditure on what she has decided to be the best weapon, she anticipates England and France.

In other words, her economical principle is the exact reverse of Lord Randolph's. She does not believe in the theory he practically laid down at Wolverhampton: "Advertise for the cheapest article; you are sure to get the best."

When, however, the question arises how the money or money's worth is originally procured from the country, we must declare that ours is by far the most economical system.

Let us take first our enormous non-effective charge, the one that has excited most the wrath of Lord Randolph and of other critics. What that charge does for us is this: it keeps all the ranks of our army from dropping into the condition of senility which attended the Royal Artillery and Royal Engineers—the only two pure seniority corps we then had—shortly before the Crimean war. How hopeless the inefficiency produced by that senility was, may be judged by any one who looks at the pathetic pictures of what a Woolwich parade was in those days. From all we have seen of the German army of late years, we much doubt whether their equivalent of our system has done as much for them. We have seen pictures of the senior officers of German messes, that might have passed for sketches taken of our officers at the worst period of our post-1815 peace-time.

But what is the German equivalent of our non-effective return? In many respects, like all other parts of the German system, it is excellent, and utilises in a very effective way the services of officers and non-commissioned officers. The State is the proprietor of all the Prussian railways, of all the Elsass-Lothringen railways, and of many more throughout the empire. Officers and non-commissioned officers, after they have retired from the army, are provided, in connection with these and other State properties, with appointments which serve as excellent substitutes for heavy pensions.

But how came the Government to be proprietor of so many railways, most of them originally started as private companies? The answer is easy, and happily illustrates the nature, on this its expensive side, of Prussian economy. The command of capital due to the French indemnity greatly facilitated the process. That vast sum was well turned over at interest, whilst it was accumulating for military purposes. The process consisted in purchasing at first a moderate number of railways that could, with the advantage of State support, be worked so sharply in competition with others that the latter no longer paid. Their proprietors were therefore glad to dispose of them at a moderate rate to the Government. The new purchase was soon turned to good account, both as a profitable investment and as a means of extending the system by competition with other railways.

In this way, no doubt, as a holder of funds, the State had arranged for their disposal at great advantage. But what about the relative cost to individuals of their system and of ours? Which would be cheaper in the long-run for English taxpayers; to pay the 2d. on the income-tax which about represents the equivalent of the cost of the non-effective return—or to have the whole railway property of the country run down by Government competition and bought up below par?

It must be remembered, in comparing the Budget of Germany with our own, that all the pensions that are paid are entirely struck off the Army Budget. So that to institute any comparison, the three millions which our non-effective vote costs must be deducted from army expenditure. The railways are only an example of the method pursued. All the offices of the State are filled with retired officers and non-commissioned officers, whose pensions are thus saved. Yet the actual monetary cost of the non-effective service of Germany is, according to General Brackenbury's evidence, £2,250,000 sterling, in addition to these salaries.

Let us take another illustration of the point we are anxious to drive home. During one of the cavalry attacks at Mars la Tour, two sons of Prince Bismarck's were riding as privates in the ranks of the 2d Dragoons of the Guards. They played their part as troopers gallantly. One was severely wounded, one carried a comrade out of fatal danger. Heaven forbid that we should disparage the moral and national advantage of such association of the highest with the lowest in the performance of simple patriotic duty! But as a question of monetary resources expended on war what does it represent? Doubtless, as far as these two young men are concerned personally, very little. It was no monetary loss to the country that they should be doing humble duty well, at a time when they were not ready for such work as has since then been given them. But as regards the number of classes between them and that which fills our ranks, what does not that simple statement imply? The agents of great mercantile houses, the eye-doctor on the Rhine with a practice of many thousands a-year, all those on whose skill and knowledge the accumulation of wealth throughout the country depended—these men were everywhere present in the ranks. Hardly any rate of taxation could extract from the country such sums of money as this complete dislocation of trade and professional work involved. Again we say, we by no means deny the gain which balanced the loss; but it was not a money gain.

We are not now dealing with that particular aspect of the case, of which Sir A. Malet, in the book we quoted in our last article, speaks when he says that the German system involves the sacrifice for almost every healthy man throughout the country of twenty years of personal independence. What we urge is, that when politicians go down among our working men, who trust them, and tell them that we are spending too much of our money, because foreign Governments do not show in their budgets sums much larger than our own, it is not enough to reply, "You forget *how cheaply* foreign Governments fill their ranks." It is not true that they fill them as cheaply as we do; though the cost to them appears in no budget. In no country in the world would the mere monetary loss of substituting a universal for a voluntary and highly paid service be so great as in our own.

To tell a nation that it is making prodigious monetary sacrifices at a time when it is in fact saving its wealth by paying those to serve whom it can best afford to employ, is to deceive it. Foreign nations sacrifice to the protection and security of national interests much more than money. They sacrifice personal ease, social privilege, individual independence. But in addition to that, they sacrifice for the whole country a power of accumulating wealth by devoting their young men to that purpose, which represents an additional monetary loss of a magnitude so enormous that the money that would be taken out of England if we adopted their methods would stand to that which we now spend in a proportion that no man can measure, but that would at least be represented by a high *multiple* of our present figure. This is the only fair method of comparison as to the money rate they are paying and the money rate we are paying for national defence.

We have spoken of the conditions of English social life as elements that must be taken into account when we try to estimate the kind of rate that must be paid if we would have economical service from those classes of which we have taken the present permanent Under-Secretary of State for War as an example. Does the same thing apply or does it not apply to our working classes?

Listen to this. Doubtless many of our readers are accustomed to read, or at least to take in, some of the agricultural journals of the country. If they do, they will bear us out when we say that a phenomenon has lately been noticed by careful observers which, like many other humble matters, has a deep significance. The markets of the country have changed in a very curious way. A few years ago, fat pigs, fat bacon, even fat mutton and fat beef, were in great demand. But farmers find that the production of fat no longer pays as it did. Why so? The answer which those give who best understand such matters is this. The vast mass of the population of these islands has acquired tastes, engendered by increasing prosperity, which make them prefer more costly ways of obtaining that necessary part of human food, of which fat is the cheapest form. Butter, butterine, and the like, are now eaten by them instead of the fat of bacon. Their very habits of cooking have changed. Moreover, though the production of fat no longer pays as it did, the consumption of bacon has increased more largely than that of any other article of commerce, because of the increased purchasing power of those who make it their chief form of meat-food.

You are thus competing for your soldiers in a market yearly offering more and more opportunities to the class from which they come of acquiring wealth, and the habits which wealth engenders. Whether, from all points of view, it is purely national gain that the population should crowd in to the work of highly paid factories, is a question beside our present purpose. What we earnestly urge upon the consideration of such politicians as Lord Randolph Churchill and Sir

Charles Dilke is this. You are actually getting your army on a system which subtracts from the general wealth of the country sums so immeasurably less than the Continental system would subtract from it, that all monetary comparisons between their budgets and ours tend to deceive us as to the sacrifices we are making.

You cannot both have your pie and eat it too. You cannot save the national purse by adopting methods which, in their direct payment for what we want, are, commercially speaking, immeasurably sounder than the Continental system of taking wealth by other means than by direct payment, and yet have an adequate defence for your vast empire by paying what they pay in hard cash.

The constant cries that ours is a most costly system are most dangerous and most deceptive. Our whole national economy is based upon commercial wisdom; and, as a mere matter of such calculation, we have been far wiser in our generation than our neighbours. But we are living in a fool's paradise. "Cut it down! cut it down!" were the cries which greeted Lord Randolph's absolutely deceptive comparison of our Army Budget and that of Germany. If you do cut it down, you can by no manner of means supply those terrible deficiencies in our needed preparation for possible war which Lord Randolph himself pointed out. Those deficiencies exist because our statesmen have been attempting an impossible problem. They have tried to adopt principles for saving the wealth of the country which do save that wealth; and yet, in comparing their doings with those of Continental statesmen, they have given themselves no credit for the saving, but have gone on to act as if they ought to get what they do not pay for.

To turn to the other side of the comparison. What has Germany to do with the army and navy which she employs? What have we with ours? The German empire lies within a ring-fence. Her system of localisation and all the cheap service which it represents is easy, because her army has, during peace-time, never to stir from home. We have an empire which occupies in mere extent one-fifth of the habitable globe, a population which is reckoned by the 100 million. But that is not all or nearly all. It is scarcely too much to say that every square mile of water which connects the outlying portions of our dominions is for us a territory needing defence as much as does Elsass-Lothringen or Pomerania. It is a defence which to be adequate needs the work alike of army and of navy; of navy first—of army, that the navy may be free to do its proper work. Everywhere over it we have harbours and fortresses, which must be held by our army unless our vast resources, dispersed over that watery dominion, are to be open to far more easy attack than any of those German villages which now sleep so securely behind the men who guard the Rhine.

Lord Randolph makes a great point of the fact that India pays for the army which we keep there, and that this is an additional proof of our extravagance. Perhaps an American general, a military Lycurgus in his own country, may be allowed the weight of an unprejudiced onlooker, so far as our Indian system is concerned. General Upton[1] has unhesitatingly declared that nowhere in all history have such results been obtained as we have secured from our native army in India. He has given all the figures of our high payments for local service, and, like Macaulay, he has declared that, judged by its results, it has been the most economical system known on earth. Those of us who know its present weaknesses know also that they all lie on the side exactly opposite to that on which Lord Randolph tries to lay his finger. If he is going to apply to India the manifold meanness suggested by his questions as chairman of his Committee, the day of the collapse of our Indian empire will date from that on which he gains power to carry out his will.

But, though our native army in India has been a marvellous and most economical accession to our imperial strength in India, and though for the

[1] See 'The Armies of Asia and Europe,' p. 75.

actual service of our European army in India that empire pays, that does not close the question as a comparison between our army and the German.

Mr Knox has perhaps by this time brought home to Lord Randolph the fact that at present the whole conditions of our service at home are determined by the necessities of our Indian and colonial empire. Even in the scheme which is now proposed for carrying out, as perfectly as may be, that sudden mobilisation the success of which in 1870, brought France down on her knees before Germany at the very opening of the campaign, the fact that our army has primarily to hold a world-wide empire must be taken into account.

We cannot have the same simple system of mobilisation as a country which keeps all its army in the neighbourhood of their homes. The continual transfer of regiments from England to India and the colonies involves, in a vast variety of ways, costs which Germany never incurs. The necessities of a voluntary service in themselves prevent its being possible to keep regiments from year to year in an unpopular station. An army which can only have to be moved by rail or road, on the outbreak of war, is on a very different footing.

We can arrange, and we are arranging, if Lord Randolph and Sir Charles Dilke will allow us to do so, to have the ports of embarkation told off for our troops, and all those conditions provided beforehand which facilitate sea-transport. The actual numbers of troops, the particular regiments the weight of their stores, will all be fixed, so that the Admiralty can at any moment know what ships will be required and what accommodation must be prepared. The stores to go on board those ships will be ready at the ports. Every reserve man will know, long beforehand, where he is to join his old regiment, and will find his clothing and equipment waiting for him on the spot. The quartering of regiments will, for the first time in our history, be arranged with a view to making easy a mobilisation either for home service or embarkation. Every item of the departments which enable an army to march and fight, which we do possess, will be turned to account. But it must be realised by Englishmen that hitherto in the hopeless attempt we have described to buy with hard cash what foreigners take by a more costly method, and yet to pay as little as they do, the English army has been hitherto always stinted of those very things on which the power of the German army depends. It was because the German army consisted, not of a number of regiments, but of *corps d'armée*, complete in all their parts, that Germany in 1870 struck down Imperial France within a month.

For though we get our money on the cheapest system we can, the Germans understand, and we do not, how to spend it when we get it. Lord Randolph and Sir Charles Dilke are agreed that they and their class have made the most hopeless mess of the process that was humanly possible. We are of the same mind. In Germany, among all the fierce attacks that have been made against Prince Bismarck and the other members of the Prussian Government, no hint has been ever dropped of a doubt that the money, once voted, has been expended in the most economical manner possible. Any one who will be at the trouble to read the questions that some of the members of the House of Commons on Lord Randolph's Committee have been asking will have no difficulty in seeing the reason why we have been in so different a condition. We have been told that the selection of the Committee has excited general dissatisfaction in the House itself. For the credit of the House of Commons, we hope that that is true. There are of course some members who always ask most business-like and excellent questions; but really others appal one. One does not expect a member of the House necessarily to know very much, but he ought at least to know where to get information. He ought to be man of the world enough not to ask a soap-manufacturer details as to the manufacture of cheese, when he is appointed to arrive at truth. Yet that is the principle on which the inquiry is being conducted.

Economy (?) in Education. 89

We heartily thank Lord Randolph for having insisted upon making public these questions as they proceed. They will supply admirable material for heckling. We commend them to the attention of constituents who have reasons of their own for wishing to make their members ridiculous when they next have to face them. Let us take an instance. Mr Knox is a most able accountant, and a most hard-working man. We suspect even Lord Randolph, if he knew nothing of him before, is a little sorry that he committed himself to the statement at Wolverhampton that the copyists did all the work at the War Office, Mr Knox and his fellows doing nothing. But Mr Knox is necessarily, like other men who achieve much in their own line, obliged to stick to his last. He does not travel far beyond the walls of the dingy, inconvenient, and poisonous office in Pall Mall, to which Lord Randolph boasts that he has confined the men on whose health and clear-headedness the efficiency of our army depends. Just imagine, then, the selecting of Mr Knox for examination on the details of the educational arrangements of the Civil Service Commissioners; on the wisdom of the arrangements of foreign armies; on the reasons why a regiment which moves from Mullingar to Stirling, then to an out-station of Plymouth, miles from any board-school, and thence to Pembroke docks, should not have its unfortunate children shunted from one board-school to another, from one absolutely different system of education to another, every time that it moves. Again, it is a tolerably familiar fact to most men who have even a little studied modern war, that the general education of the German army has been one of its greatest powers. Our own conviction of the relative weakness of the Russian army is based on the stolid ignorance of the Russian peasantry. Nothing has so much tended of late years to increase the practical power of our own army as its enforced education. No one who knows what a young soldier is when he first joins would dream of submitting to him the question whether he would like to learn. A greater cruelty could not be done him. Every temptation is thrown in his way not to learn. If the option is nominally left to him, it will be no option at all. All weak young fellows will yield to the pressure of their comrades, and will avoid learning. In most regiments the question—the vital question—of whether they can or can not get good non-commissioned officers is almost absolutely a question of whether their commanding officers have or have not taken pains to encourage the general education of their recruits.

Yet these gentlemen select Mr Knox, who can by no accident have had either the experience or the special knowledge of the conditions of modern war, required to answer such a question, as *the* man whose opinion they take on the point whether money may not be saved by making optional the regimental schools for the privates, as well as of doing away with the other educational establishments of the army. There are numbers of English soldiers whose special business it has been to make themselves acquainted with the conditions of foreign armies. If their own evidence is to be distrusted because they are soldiers, they at least know to what unanswerable and authoritative documents the Committee ought to be referred. But if the soldiers are to be examined on the technical details of army accounts as carried on in the War Office, and the accountants on questions of pure military experience, what result but miserable failure can come of this wretched system of inquiry?

This is the sort of economy which in the past has been so costly. "Happy thought," says some one who knows nothing about it. "Let us do away with the expense of the education of the army. Soldiers want to fight, not to learn. They would like it ever so much better themselves.' Slap goes the vote. Two years after appear some powerful letters from a newspaper correspondent, pointing out how all-important in modern war the education of some foreign army has proved in a decisive campaign, in which public interest at the time is absorbed. Everything must then be sacrificed to the one object of educating the soldier. Money is voted to repurchase land and buildings, and to re-establish a machinery which cannot be made as efficient as the old one that was destroyed. Everything is at high pressure and double cost.

We take this as an illustration. Hitherto, we must admit, education has not been assailed. But Lord Randolph will, no doubt, easily persuade the men of Wolverhampton that no one ought to know anything that they do not; so that now the special turn of education has come. In other matters—in those on which the military power, the sudden striking power more especially of Germany and now of France too depend—we have been doomed to impotence by the hopelessness of attempting to make the House of Commons interested in army efficiency. Whatever attracted attention—the talk of ladies looking on from the House of Commons' stand at a great review—has had its due favour. Those things, the value of which the experience of war alone can teach, have been left to take their chance.

Hence it happens that while we have for our army the infantry, cavalry, and artillery, for those two corps of which we have spoken we are without any adequate supply of the needed transport, of the needed medical staff, of the needed engineers for bridging, for telegraph work, and for other engineer duties. We have no supply ready of the field-bakeries, of "artillery ammunition columns," or "infantry ammunition columns," or "provision columns."

Now, in the German army all these bodies in their due proportion are embodied in, and form part of, the mobilisation of each *corps d'armée*.

This is the great contrast which must strike any one who will be at the trouble of turning to the Appendix of the Prussian official history of the war of 1870 and comparing the tabular statement of the German army with our own army estimates, or with any other complete record of our army as it exists. If the various portions of the force which are there given had ever existed in our army, they would long since have been abolished, because some one would have asked Mr Knox why such unwarlike agents should be kept up in peace-time? It is not Mr Knox's business to know the answer; but Mr Knox's authority would have been sufficient for their abolition.

Now, from the German point of view, economy consists in providing those things which make an army efficient. Our own army is not efficient for war, and cannot be ready to take the field with that rapidity which is of the essence of the question, until we can, on the word "mobilise" being issued from headquarters, instantly prepare whatever force we have complete in all these respects.

To send an army into the field unprovided with

those auxiliary aids, without which an army cannot move, without which it cannot fight, is as reasonable as to send a regiment into the field without its arms. If the question were whether we should send to war one regiment armed with the best breech-loaders or two unarmed at all, no one would hesitate as to the answer. Yet to any one who has studied modern war it is just as wise, it amounts to the same thing, to send an army into the field without its proper auxiliary services, thinking that you add more to its force by increasing its cavalry, infantry, and artillery without supplying what you have with what is required to enable them to fight, as to keep on adding to an army men whom you cannot arm.

The central cause of this enormous difference between the wisdom with which the German money once obtained for war is administered, and the folly with which we expend ours, lies in the existence in Berlin of that "great staff," of which Von Moltke is the head. Until quite lately we have had no body whatever in London which supplied the place of that "great staff." The "Horse Guards" and "War Office" are employed on matters of daily routine and petty detail—very largely, indeed, in preparing answers for questions put forward in the House of Commons to embarrass a Government for party purposes. Von Moltke's staff does not concern itself at all with the innumerable matters of minor regimental discipline the solution of which is the chief duty of the Adjutant-General's Department of our army. It is absorbed entirely in the consideration of those matters on which the effective fighting power of the army depends. Of late these have with us been undertaken by the Intelligence Department. That department is a kind of parasite. Its absolute necessity and its value has made itself so felt by all other departments, not only of the War Office but of the Government, that it has gradually been absorbing duties almost analogous to those of the "great staff"; but it is in its wrong place. It ought to be the thinking head of the army—that which deals under the immediate responsibility of the chief of the army with all the questions of the mode in which the money vote by Parliament can be most economically and efficiently used—the questions of organisation, the questions of preparedness for war. The mighty questions whether a private in an infantry regiment ought or ought not to have been punished for going to sleep in church, whether a corporal's guard should or should not have been relieved at two o'clock, and the like, with which actually now the time of a man like Lord Wolseley is not unfrequently occupied, ought to be dealt with, on their own responsibility and finally, long before the Horse Guards is reached.

Our present system of centralisation does not

confer power on the headquarters of the army. It deprives them of all real power by burying them under detail. We have a congress of departments at headquarters; we have a congress of regiments and of local staffs about the country. We have no "great general staff;" we have no *corps d'armée*.

II. *The New Military Frontiers of Germany and of France.*—We turn now to the second question with which we proposed to deal: The relative military power of Germany and of France, and more especially the respective strength of their two frontiers. Simultaneously with our last article, whilst we were expressing our conviction that Sir Charles Dilke was in error in maintaining the superior strength for practical purposes of the French and Russian frontiers over the German, an article appeared in the 'Contemporary Review,' written by a German officer, which, so far as the actual fortifications of France against Germany and of Germany against France are concerned, leaves nothing to be desired. We are the better pleased that that should be so, because we are anxious to avoid a vast body of detailed geographical description, and a catalogue of names, which, for all but a limited class of readers, would possess neither meaning nor interest. For all details, therefore, of the most elaborate system of French defence, we may refer our readers to that article.

What we desire to do is to explain the broad principles on which the two most opposite systems of defence, carried out by the two nations, have been designed, and to give our reasons for preferring to believe in the German. After the war of 1870, the French engineers found that, with the exception of a very small strip of the frontier, the Germans had possessed themselves of the old natural mountain-barrier on which France had for generations relied for her defence. They had to deal with a country not in itself strongly defensible. They had virtually a *tabula rasa* on which to exercise their skill. They have worked with the greatest ability, backed by an unstinted supply of money. Incredible as the sum appears, France is reputed to have expended since 1870 on her re-armament and fortification 135 *million pounds sterling*. Such a sum skilfully expended could not fail to produce a formidable result. They have piled fortification upon fortification all along the frontier. Certainly he would be a rash man who would venture to speak confidently as to the result, should the German armies have to attack this continuous belt of fortification, adequately garrisoned by formidable troops.

Belfort itself has been girdled with forts. Epinal has been similarly strengthened, so has Toul, so has Verdun. A great defensive position has been prepared on the "Plateau de Haye," between Frouard and Pont St Vincent. Then curtains of *forts d'arrêt* close all the chief roads between these great places of defence. An elaborate series of defences cover the Côtes de Meuse between Toul and Verdun. In second line Langres, Besançon, and Dijon have been converted into vast intrenched camps. In fact, as Major Wachs says, Epinal, Belfort, Besançon, Dijon, and Langres form a large strategic pentagon, in which every angle is filled with a fortified place of the first rank. Reims, La-Fère, and Laon have all been converted into intrenched camps. So numerous are the forts which connect these various greater places that only two gaps of any extent remain, one between Verdun and the Belgian frontier, one between Toul and Epinal. These have been deliberately left in order to tempt an invader to advance by lines which would be disadvantageous to him. Nor is this all; the network of railways in rear of these fortresses, and connecting them, is most elaborate and complete.

The enormous size of the works may be judged by the fact that Verdun will require a garrison of 25,000 men to hold it; it has for its external forts a perimeter of 27½ miles, Epinal has similarly a perimeter of 28 miles, Belfort of 30 miles—and so on.

Before discussing what appears to us to be the weak point in this magnificent scheme, let us consider what Germany has done on the other side.

First, she has demolished nearly all the smaller forts and fortresses in Elsass-Lothringen. Secondly, she has everywhere elaborated her facilities for detraining and entraining troops. She has perfected her railway communication between all parts of Germany where corps assemble, and Strasbourg and Metz. She has also perfected the railway system north and south, as well as east and west, within the newly conquered territory. Thirdly, she has made of Strasbourg with Kehl an intrenched camp so vast, that Major Wachs declares—and we believe that it is true though others scarcely put the figures so high—that it would cover and supply an army of 280,000 men. It can be protected by a belt of water from the Ill, the Rhone Canal, and the Rhine. Three of the forts are similarly protected by wet ditches. The forts communicate by subterranean telegraph wires, and a railway circuit connects them with the great system of railway which converges on Strasbourg. We rather doubt Major Wachs' statement that this circular railway is now in order, but the roadway is there, and the rails could easily be laid down. Germany has enormously improved and strengthened the forts round Metz. She has treated with a sort of careless indifference three other fortresses which she has not actually dismantled, Thionville, Bitsch, and Saarlouis.

By the treaty after the war, she obtained possession also of Neu Breisach, and this she has retained in its old form, as it covers an important bridge over the Rhine. Here, as elsewhere, she has greatly improved the facilities for detraining troops. Breisach will serve to bring into the Southern Vosges the Bavarian corps. But, with the exceptions we have named, no other fortresses have been left standing on the French side beyond the line of the Rhine. Germany has, however, still her old line of great intrenched camps, giving her command of rivers—Ulm, Rastatt, Mayence, Coblentz, Cologne, and Wesel.

She has over the Rhine itself no fewer than sixteen railway bridges, besides four steam ferries, capable of carrying entire trains, and also twenty bridges of boats for wheeled carriages. Most of these passages are fortified. All can be rapidly destroyed. Double lines of railway run along either bank of the Rhine throughout its entire length.

Now what does this mean? It means that Germany relies for the defence of her territory against France upon facilitating in every way the gathering of her forces upon the French frontier, and upon striking in the field rapid blows against any French force that shall attempt to pass the Rhine to invade her. It means that every topographical condition which will hamper the movement of an army attempting rapid offence against her has been studied; that she will have the most telling bases and pivots of manœuvre for supplying her forces. The Germans will be able to manœuvre in concentrated masses against an enemy who must expose himself to blows in such fashion that the German army can strike on flanks or rear. The blow may be delivered when the French army is divided by the necessities of movement in difficult country or across a great river, of which the Germans hold all the bridges, so that they can forbid its passage to the French and pass it themselves when and where they please. That is the nature of the defence manifestly designed.

It is as auxiliary to this purpose that the great camps exist. Her army is not swallowed up by many fortresses. The great mass of the fortresses which we have named, which hold the rivers, are far to the rear, so that, whilst the active army moves forward to the frontier, there can gather securely behind them the great territorial army, which will fill these camps, and be daily gaining cohesion and discipline.

And now as to what she will do for offence. That clearly depends on the weak spot she has the opportunity to assail. In all that vast and wonderful mass of fortification which confronts her, is there one? Not in the fortresses, perhaps, as yet; but, unless all that we have gathered from the discussions which have of late been sufficiently ample in France, and from some other sources, be deceptive, there will be one most serious weakness involved in the French system of defence.

Among the literature which poured from the French press after the war of 1870-71, there was one pathetic little pamphlet, written by the Emperor of the French himself, describing the causes of the French disasters. He emphatically declared that the great cause of all his trouble was that neither he nor any one else understood that the movement of troops by railway for a great campaign was an art in itself, till the bitter experience of war taught him how little he knew about it. The statement was certainly an exaggerated one. The causes of the woes of France lay much deeper than that. But this much is certain, that everything for France in the next war with Germany will at first depend on the question whether her soldiers have or have not practically mastered the difficulty which the methodic movement to the frontier of both her active and territorial army will entail upon her.

For the defect of that vast agglomeration of works which she has piled together is, that it will take an army to defend it. Germany, with her one strong place of Metz, fronts ten first-class fortresses alone, independent of all the minor forts which jostle one another along that mighty line. If the French proposed to employ their regular army

in these works, well might Major Wachs exclaim, as he does: "Now, this riveting of an army to a fixed immovable spot is difficult to combine with the offensive, and the year 1870 showed that a French army could be brought rapidly behind walls, but not easily before them; so that we may be permitted to ask the question, Whether the nation which leads so excited a life to the west of the Vosges is still the same that in former times used to be so eager to advance and attack the enemy, and which, indeed, always showed a rapture for open battle and swift decision, and the profoundest aversion to merely standing and exchanging fire, or to remaining long behind wall and trench?
. . . Dead walls are the grave-stones of the military self-confidence of the French, and the 'notwithstanding their presence,' may very soon be converted into 'because of their presence.' France prefers to put her trust in the shield rather than in the hand that wields the spear."

But Major Wachs, carefully as he has studied the French frontier, evidently does not know the French views as to the mode in which these fortresses are to be held. The idea is that, whilst the active army takes the field, these fortresses are to be occupied by the territorial army. There seems to us to lie the weakness of the whole scheme. It appears to have escaped notice in England that France has never ventured to adopt the system of localisation and territorial mobilisation of the Germans. When the word "mobilise" goes forth from the French headquarters, the reserves which will join the nearest troops will not be the men who have been trained with the regiments they join. It is extremely difficult to believe that such an operation can be conducted with the rapidity, ease, and certainty with which a German village, in which all the men belong to one company, falls in and joins the men of the next village or two in making up the total reserves of the battalion whose headquarters lie close to them. It is very difficult not to believe that the French will suffer as we have done ourselves from the want of cohesion, due to vast numbers of men being placed with officers they have not known before. Then the whole mass of men, both of the active and territorial army, will have to move eastwards. The army will have to take up its position; the territorial force to occupy the forts. It is the most enormous problem of military railway transport under the most difficult conditions that has been ever attempted. It may succeed, of course; but, during all the earlier years which followed 1870, if not since then, there was an irregularity and uncertainty about the way in which men were passed into the reserves and about the way in which the training was given, which makes us gravely doubt whether the mobilisation will not be much more like that which

Prussia attempted in 1849 and in 1859, which collapsed, rather than like that of 1866 or 1870. Practice makes perfect rather in such matters as these than in most others. It was no bellicose wish which induced General Boulanger to desire the experimental mobilisation of two corps. At all events, whatever may have been his private views, there was grave reason why France should make the experiment. We have solid grounds for believing that, shortly prior to his proposal for the mobilisation of the corps, General Boulanger had specifically ascertained that all arrangements for the movements by railway of the French army on a large scale were in a condition as chaotic as they had been prior to the war of 1870. If that is true, we would give very little for the value to France of the 135 millions spent on the fortifications.[1]

For what, meantime, has Germany been doing as regards her own mobilisation? The one arm of the service which in 1870 was relatively slow in being ready was the one whose services were needed first—the cavalry. If we are rightly informed, such vigorous steps have been taken to remedy that inconvenience, that, thirty-six hours after the magic word "mobilise" has arrived, each cavalry regiment will be ready to take the field.

[1] I do not think that the mobilisation actually dispelled these causes for suspicion. It was known too long beforehand which corps was to be mobilised, and the difficulties described above could not in the experiment have occurred.

Everything is done in Germany with a silence which contrasts notably with the chatter and the fussy efforts at secrecy which were characteristic of General Boulanger's administration. It is therefore not easy to be certain to what point the time required for mobilisation has been actually reduced. It is put sometimes now as low as four days. The maximum time is, we believe, at all events, six days. After that, it will be simply a question of extremely rapid railway transport upon fortified places for large portions, at least, of the army. Without knowing the total number of entraining and detraining stations available for each corps, it would be impossible to estimate the time within which the German army may be reckoned upon to arrive within striking distance of the French line. It is upon such points as these, the amount of rolling-stock and the multiplication of railway lines, and not upon mere distance, that the rate of transfer of large bodies of troops depends. Seeing that the German Government has been bending all its energies to facilitate movement by these means ever since the war, we confess that we anticipate a rapidity of concentration on the frontier or on the Rhine that will startle the world almost as much as the earlier successes of 1870 surprised it. If that confusion reigns over the French mobilisation which we anticipate, so that, at the moment when the German forces are ready on their frontier, the occupation of the French frontier forts is in progress, or if the forts are occupied by inferior troops hurriedly brought together, that will be the moment of the German stroke. The two forts which must be taken in order to enable a German army to advance will be suddenly attacked and overwhelmed with fire. That their capture will cost the Germans severe loss in men cannot be doubted. But it must be remembered that under all conditions of warfare that we have ever known, the weakness of a practically continuous and greatly extended system of fortification lies in this, that broken in one point it is broken in all. *Mutatis mutandis*, the example of Marlborough's success against the very same system when adopted by the French of his day will apply now. The danger to the French lies in the temptation which Mr Hooper, in his lately published history of the Sedan campaign, very ably discusses as that which will be held out to weak commanders of an exaggerated reliance on great intrenched camps. We agree with his critic in the 'Spectator' that the case of Metz and Bazaine is not fairly in point; because Metz, as it existed in 1870, did not fulfil any of the conditions which obtain in either the French or German camps of to-day. But, nevertheless, the danger is a real one. No one who has followed our statement will fail to see how anxiously the Germans have endeavoured to avoid it. There is no mistaking the significance of their careful demolition of Schlettstadt, Marsal, Phalsbourg, La Petite Pierre, Lichtenberg, and Landau.

As Major Wachs has put it in the passage we have quoted, the danger is lest an army " brought rapidly behind walls" will not be brought " easily before them." For our own part, we have the most profound belief in the strength of a defensive position under the modern conditions of war; provided always that an army knows how, when needed, to use it, and when to dispense with it. But that local power of the defensive is one which a skilful assailant may turn to his own profit, as the Germans showed alike before Metz, Sedan, and Paris. The French method is, as Major Wachs has well said, a recurrence to the " cordon system of the last century." Beyond doubt the completeness in itself of each separate fortification is a matter of the greatest importance ; but we confess to thinking that there is risk lest these fortifications should be only too comfortable for the generals of the French army. Victory will now, as ever, be ultimately decided in the open field. Fortifications are of importance in so far as they assist an army in its operations in the field. They become dangerous when, instead of being used as pivots of manœuvre, they are erected, like the stone wall of China, themselves to bar the progress of the invader.

We think that, in what we have said, we have supplied an explanation, and to some extent even a justification, of Sir Charles Dilke's statement, though we have given our reasons for differing from him. To any one looking merely at the elaboration, the cost, the completeness of the French defence, it must seem that the Germans have on their side done nothing comparable to it. The German behaves like the master of fence who apparently drops his point, and lays his breast open to be stabbed. Woe betide the unskilful fencer who thinks that he has also dropped his eye!

III. *Will the Germans violate Belgian territory?*—It will, perhaps, now be apparent why we do not ourselves believe that Germany will make her great attempt upon France by violating Belgian territory. We have no wish to speak dogmatically on the subject. We are quite aware that others, whose judgment is entitled to the greatest weight, think differently. For our own part we believe distinctly that Sir Charles Dilke has done the greatest service to Belgium in drawing her attention to the necessity that,

"Would she be free, herself should strike the blow."

But, as it seems to us, the balance of advantage to Germany in moving by that line is so nice a one, that a conviction that Belgium and England would act together to resist any such attempt would be amply sufficient to turn the scale. If Belgium refuses to play her part in maintaining her neutrality, the case falls of course. We are under no obligation to assist her if she will spend nothing on the armaments and the men that are needed to fulfil her international contract. We certainly should be most unwilling to say anything that may tend to prevent Belgium from setting her house in order. But if we are right as to the weak point in the French defence at which it is the policy of Germany to strike, it is obvious that the blow must be struck rapidly and in an unknown direction. Time is of the essence of the question. Now for Germany to choose the road by Belgium is to abandon all the advantages of time.

It is as well to remember that during the war of 1870 and in the advance on Sedan, subsequent that is to the negotiation of our common treaty with Germany and France for the protection of Belgium during August of that year, orders were given to the German army that "should the enemy enter Belgian territory and not be disarmed at once, he is to be followed thither without delay."[1] Obviously we should in that case have had even under that treaty no *casus belli* against Germany. The case is analogous to that of a blockade, which,

[1] Prussian Official History, vol. ii. p. 291.

to be respected, must be effective. In speaking, therefore, of German violation of Belgian territory, we speak of direct invasion intended to attack the northern frontier of France, so as to avoid the necessity of dealing with the great fortress barrier between Verdun and Belfort. We do not speak of such chance violation of territory as may occur in any marches made to the north of Verdun in the course of a westerly movement. If that frontier of Belgium be not properly guarded, it will no doubt be casually or deliberately violated by parties on both sides. We doubt, in that case, if anything but diplomatic apologies, more or less sincere, could be expected to follow.

When we speak of the element of time being against a German invasion of France by way of Belgium, we speak of an advance from Cologne across Belgian territory, directed upon Mézières and Maubeuge, either to turn the line of the fortresses or to carry the army immediately upon Paris. At Metz, and in the general concentration in Elsass-Lothringen, the German armies can, within their own territory, concentrate by railway without its being possible for any but the vaguest reports to reach the French as to the direction of the impending blow. They arrive at once without difficulty within striking distance, and with all the facilities so necessary to a railway concentration afforded by terminal stations elaborately prepared for the purpose. The nearest point at which concentration can take place on similar terms on the Belgian frontier is at Aix-la-Chapelle. From Aix only a single railway runs across the frontier of Belgium. Obviously, if force were attempted on this side, it would be the duty of the Belgian Government to destroy this line. As the crow flies, the distance from Aix to Mézières is ninety miles; and as the railway runs through Liège, and makes a considerable detour, it would be impossible for any Prussian force to secure it throughout its length without deliberate connivance or scandalous neglect on the part of the Belgians. Even were the line in the hands of the Germans it would furnish a most insecure dependence for supply. At best the army must march by road through Belgium, so that at least six or seven days must elapse between the departure from Aix and the arrival within striking distance of the French frontier. Six or seven days of clear warning would thus be given to the French before their first line of defence could be reached.

Though the defences of the northern frontier of France are not like those of the eastern, they are not to be despised. Here the character of the French defence much more nearly approaches to that of the German, as we have already discussed it. The railways would facilitate the rapid gathering of the armies from all parts of France. Their movement thither would not interfere with the concentration eastwards of the territorial army into the great fortress belt. The main line of supply for the German armies would still be intercepted by the Verdun-Belfort forest of fortresses. It seems to us inconceivable that, if this Belgian line alone were taken, the French armies should not be able to meet the German in superior numbers, in more perfect concentration, and with every advantage of position in their favour.

Of course the case would present fresh complications if the neutrality of Luxembourg were violated as well as that of Belgium. Again here we must say that the question mainly turns upon the sincere desire of the King of Holland to fulfil international obligation. By an agreement with the King of Holland, no doubt the railway from Tréves by Luxembourg and Arlon could be made to assist; but to any one who realises what the nature of a great railway movement of thousands of men and their stores is, it will, we think, be evident that the mere fact of this violation of territory would at once and necessarily substitute marching by road for railway shipment, at least for the first advance of the troops. Probably, in any case, in order to relieve the railways, parts of the German army from the nearer distances will march. But the developed facilities for railway transport since the war are now so great that it does not look as if, for the first line of their main army, that were the German purpose.

By no manner of means that we can see would it be possible for a German army to maintain itself in France and to carry out successfully an offensive campaign, unless some part of the great fortress barrier is by one means or another broken down, Certainly it would be impossible without a preliminary complete and absolute conquest of Belgium and possession of Luxembourg, unless the barrier be broken. Therefore, as it seems to us that the easiest time for breaking that barrier will be the earliest possible moment at which it can be attempted, and as it cannot be done so quickly by moving on the northern frontier as by striking boldly at the eastern, we do not believe that the tendency of the military situation lies in the direction of invasion of France by Germany through Belgium. Either the condition of a preliminary attempt of France to adopt that line, or absolute quiescence and indifference to her liberties on the part of Belgium, would no doubt materially alter the whole aspect of the case.

As long ago as in 1868-69, Von Moltke pronounced decisively as to the advantages to the French of not violating Swiss or Belgian territory. To any one who reads his words now, it will, we think, be tolerably evident that with very little modification the same argument applies both to

French and German action under present conditions:—

"The neutrality of Belgium, Holland, and Switzerland limits the theatre of war to the area between Luxemburg and Basle. Should France disregard the neutrality of one of these States—say Belgium—her army must weaken itself considerably in Brussels and before Antwerp. Her further advance over the Meuse can be more effectively met from the Moselle than from Cologne, as we should compel the enemy to form front to the south, and whilst threatening his communications, give him decisive battle. As the distance from Brussels to Cologne is greater than from either Maintz, Kaiserslautern, or Trier, we should, in such an eventuality, still be in time to take up a position on our lower Rhine front.

"No less difficulties would ensue were France to violate the neutrality of Switzerland, in which country she would have to encounter a strong and well-organised militia.

"Now, the concentration of considerable forces on the Moselle would so immediately threaten France and her capital, that she could hardly embark in such very remote enterprises."[1]

Of all possible violations of territory, that which appears to us to be by far the most probable, if any is attempted, is that of Switzerland by France

[1] Prussian Official History, Part I., vol. i. p. 51.

in the event of a war in which, from the fact of Germany being engaged against another powerful enemy, France became the invader. Von Moltke has given the reasons which make even that improbable; but certainly our experience during the last fifty years does not tend to show that Swiss neutrality has been much respected. Nevertheless, though the southern frontier of Germany lies almost absolutely unguarded, though few troops are quartered there, and the railway system is most incomplete, Germany looks upon the danger to France of throwing into the scale against herself the hostility of Switzerland, as a point sufficiently important to enable Germany to disregard the menace of the many fortresses and the accumulation of men ready for action which, on the French side, front Switzerland. We say this only to point out how, when forces are so nicely balanced as they are at present on the Continent, politics must determine the course of war rather than the necessities of war determine the course of politics. The Germans boast that with them it is for the soldiers to tackle the problem, subject to the necessary political conditions. They will not draw into the scale against Germany one little State, whose hostility might be inconvenient, in order to ease the military problem, or to seem to ease it.

Therefore we say boldly, that if the question

remains doubtful whether Belgium, doing her duty to Europe, shall be abandoned to the strong arm of violence, it is within the power of England, if she possesses the strength, without which she cannot guard her own empire, to decide the issue. The Netherlands, Belgium, and England together, would certainly not be "*une quantité négligible*" [1] for either France or Germany. Neither Power would attempt, during a war with the other, to place on their direct line of communication such forces as could thus be thrown against them. The risk, in a military sense, would be far too serious. If Belgium arms, and England forbids violation of her territory, the territory of Belgium will not be violated.

IV. *Has England abandoned Belgium?*—Therefore it is important to examine the grounds on which Sir Charles Dilke expresses his conviction that all England has changed its mind since 1870.

There was a letter of "Diplomaticus" in the 'Standard,' there was an article in the 'Standard,' and we know not what other anonymous paper or two, written by some, we do not use the word in any offensive sense, literary hack or other performing his morning's task. This is Sir Charles Dilke's

---

[1] The phrase, it will be remembered, used by French statesmen in reference to the power of China, before Tonquin taught a different lesson.

view of public opinion. There are two authorities to whom we at present and in the first instance propose to appeal against him. The first is that masterly statement in the first volume of Kinglake's 'Crimea,' of the way in which action and reaction set in, in public opinion in England. Such nothings as those of which Sir Charles speaks almost always catch some back current of the uninformed public mind. We cannot believe that the influence of a man, no matter how able he may be, writing anonymously, as Sir Charles Dilke did, in a magazine, is so great that he has power to evoke immediately an informed and final expression of the purpose and will of England. England is a great country, and before its mind is definitely declared, some precedent thrashing out of a question is needed. The materials for forming its judgment must be laid before it. We feel very little doubt that Sir Charles Dilke did good service in raising the question. We disbelieve that he has received the final answer, which will be given when all the data have been laid before those from whom England learns to judge of war and politics. We prefer to believe with Lord Salisbury that the determination of what England will do in the future is to be judged rather by the whole course of past English history and politics than by the chance opinions of a particular politician.

Let us then hear how English feeling was actually expressed when the question last came before it. Lord Granville was at the time our Foreign Minister. It happened, therefore, that the following scene took place in the House of Lords. It would not have mattered at the time in what assembly of Englishmen the question had been raised, the result would have been the same.

Lord Russell had just declared in relation to the defence of Belgium, "that it was impossible to conceive a more specific and defined obligation than ours. We are bound to defend Belgium." Other speakers on both sides of the House had spoken in the same tone. In reply: "With the general and enthusiastic cheers of the House, Lord Granville made the required declaration. 'I venture,' he said, 'to state most positively, that her Majesty's Government are not unaware of the duty which this country owes to the independence and the neutrality of Belgium;' and, 'I trust that, whatever may be the opinion of individual members of this House, your lordships will not believe that when once we have made a clear intimation of our intentions in any respect, anything will prevent us from adhering scrupulously to the position we have taken.'"

We confess that the wording of Lord Granville's speech seems to us to put the matter on grounds which would make us very unwilling to believe that England would easily abandon a duty of such distinct obligation as this. Observe the indignant repudiation of the idea that an English Government could be supposed to be guilty of such treachery; the implied sense not only of the entire House, but of the entire country, that, however unpleasant the duty, it was one that we could not shirk.[1] We can only suppose that the sense of helplessness in presence of the great forces of the Continent has in the minds of some writers engendered the idea that we cannot attempt to fulfil a plain international duty. For our own part we believe that the Sibyl will be inexorable, and will demand a higher price, and offer less for it, every time that we refuse to pay what she asks as the condition of empire. Both France and Germany are only too anxious that they should have data on which they can depend, and would welcome our boldly insisting on the sacredness of the soil of Belgium. Indeed, according to the "conclusion" of Sir Charles Dilke's now published volume, he

[1] As a study of controversial method, it is worth noting that Sir Charles Dilke's reference to this passage is to say that I "quoted Lord Russell against him." It will be seen that the reference to Lord Russell is most casual, merely in order to lead up to Lord Granville's speech in behalf of Mr Gladstone's Cabinet, given "with the general and enthusiastic cheers of the House," and expressly cited as an illustration of the universal feeling of the country. Sir Charles Dilke, however, could, under present circumstances, afford to sneer at Lord Russell, not at Lord Granville, hence this method of citation.

has been severely handled in France, because of the curiously false reading of his articles that he himself advocated the abandonment of Belgium. Certainly a previous announcement of our intention to play so paltry a part would help to bring about the evil.

V. *The French and German Armies of to-day.*—When, apart from the mere question of frontier, we balance or attempt to balance the present forces of Germany and France, the problem is a far more difficult and more complex one. On the one hand, seventeen years is a long period in the history of armies. It is the period between the Napoleon of 1798 and the Napoleon of Waterloo. It is the period between the Prussia of the "Political Capitulation of Olmütz" and the Prussia of Sadowa. It is ten years more than the period between the collapse of the Prussian mobilisation of 1859 and the mobilisation which overthrew the German Confederation. As far, therefore, as time is concerned, there is no reason whatever why the weights should not have changed in the scales. The power of armies is a thing which cannot be gauged by any sight. Moreover, the seventeen years that have passed have strangely enough just added those years to the age of the elderly men who commanded the German armies in 1870, and have left them still in authority. Unless we are much misinformed, a tendency of this kind towards a too great senility has to some extent tended to invade all ranks of officers. Few things are more ruinous to the efficiency of an army. Indeed, if the German army had been like the Prussia of Frederick the Great, or the France of Napoleon, or even the English army of Wellington, resting on the traditions of a great name, we should, from analogy, incline to suspect that the chances of its having suffered very seriously in efficiency from the lapse of time were very strong indeed. But the peculiarity of the campaign of 1870 was that, able leader as Von Moltke showed himself, it was not he who won most of the battles. It was the German army. Mr Hooper, to whose work we have already referred, has admirably pointed out both the dangers and the power which attended the mode in which the Germans fought their battles. The risks which would have been run by them if the numbers and other conditions had been anything like equal, are beyond dispute. But for all that, the trained habit of war, the knowledge how to act together in emergencies, the mutual confidence, represented a force of its kind unique and new. Some approach to it existed formerly in our own army in the Peninsula. But the conditions of 1870 demanded a far freer exercise of individual initiative than was ever possible before. Hence one may almost say that it was the engrained habits or custom of the German army which won the war, or at least gave to the Germans the marvellous power they developed. Now there are few things in the world more permanent than custom. We incline, therefore, to believe that the efficiency of the German army is likely to be maintained for a far longer time than has usually happened where armies formed under the ideas of a great leader have rusted during a long peace, and have gradually mistaken forms for the spirit which once animated them. That certainly is a danger for the German army, but we do not think that it has yet affected it. The conviction which we feel in looking at a set of German soldiers at work is still always that whatever has to be done is done with absolute thoroughness and efficiency.

On the other side, we cannot persuade ourselves that all the gaseous froth which has attended the career of General Boulanger was precisely the thing that was wanted to give efficiency to the French army. To take a small point. There was a great flourish of trumpets a little time ago as to the supply to the French army of magazine rifles. So far as we can ascertain, few divisions have actually received them. Meantime, beyond all doubt and question, the German Government, which has talked as little as possible about the matter, has been steadily proceeding with the actual armament. In the same way, everywhere one gets a sense that the French will have talked of a good deal more than they have done, and that the Germans will have done a good deal more than they have talked about. That affects largely the question even of the armed forces that will respectively be put into the field.

The grand French total shows, on paper, a force of 646,000 odd more men than the German,—the German total being 2,075,000, the French 2,721,000.[1] If a great leader, capable of awaking the enthusiasm of the French, should arise, there is, of course, no calculating what influence that fact might have on the future war; but that at present the general temper of the French army, and more especially of the territorial army, represents the same high condition as the German, we cannot persuade ourselves. Probably the territorial army is now better in hand than were those Gardes Mobiles who surprised MacMahon by demanding to be sent back to Paris instead of towards Berlin; but with such an enormous operation to be carried out, as is represented by the mobilisation, the very numbers that will come to hand must depend on the discipline of men scattered all over the country. We cannot satisfy ourselves that the indications are that the discipline of the French army is in a satisfactory condition. That, with such elaborate

[1] This is balanced by the new German bill.

preparations as the French have made, the war would be a very different one from that of 1870, we have no doubt; but that at present the German army would still be able to give a good account of the French we feel tolerably certain. The element of self-confidence, so necessary to the French, which made the French Guards, always accustomed to victory, go forward with such power during the 1870 campaign, has disappeared. The French are always talking to persuade themselves that they are as good or better than the Germans. The talk sounds hollow. It has not in it that kind of ring which presages victory. The Germans have acquired a calm confidence which they did not possess at the beginning of 1870.

We must leave for our two next articles an examination of the bearing of these remarks upon the general question of the balance of power as it affects ourselves. It will be necessary to consider, first, the Russo-German frontiers and their effect on possible war.

Note.—A courteous and friendly critic of our last article in the 'St James's Gazette' suggests a doubt whether it was not Sir Arthur Otway, and not Mr Bright, who caused the removal of the term the "balance of power in Europe" from the Mutiny Act. We are grateful to him for giving us an excuse for citing a rather curious and interesting piece of historical evidence from a friend who, on the appearance of the last article, wrote to us,—" It may interest you to know that I happened to be in the Speaker's Gallery of the House of Commons when Mr Bright came to speak to a friend of his who was sitting near me, and said to him, 'Do you know, I have just found out the oddest thing in the world. Would you believe that they have retained to this year the statement that our army is maintained "for the preservation of the balance of power in Europe"?' They both laughed, and next year the words disappeared from the Army List."

Our own statement was founded upon a letter from Mr Bright to a friend which we well remember to have seen published at the time. We do not remember the exact part which Sir Arthur Otway may have played in the matter, but that the Cabinet Minister whose action determined the change was Mr Bright, we believe to be beyond dispute.

We do not know whether it is necessary to point out to more than one reader of our last article, that we certainly did not say that Mr Bradlaugh was the author of the very ancient form of adjuration "By Jingo"; but that we did say that he invented the political nickname "A Jingo," "The Jingoes," founding it upon the then popular song in which the ancient adjuration appeared. As a correspondent of the 'Glasgow Herald' thinks that he has disposed of our statement by quoting from 'Bombastes Furioso' the oath, we may say, first, that he might have seen from our own article that the use of the oath in the popular song preceded Mr Bradlaugh's use of the political nickname; and, secondly, that the antiquity of the oath runs many centuries back before 'Bombastes Furioso.' Our assertion as to the authorship of the nickname has not been challenged, because it could not be.

III.

GERMANY, RUSSIA, AND AUSTRIA

I

GERMANY, RUSSIA, AND AUSTRIA.

IT happened to the present writer to be in Paris almost immediately after the fall of the Commune in 1871. Both then and at a rather later period, whilst M. Thiers was still the ruling power in France, he was staying with French friends who had means of knowing what the private views and private conversation of that veteran statesman were. Again and again he was assured that M. Thiers was bent upon preparing France to be ready for two events—the death of the present Emperor of Germany, and the death of the then Tzar. There is surely something pathetic in the case. The one factor of which elderly men seem never to take account is the uncertainty of the space within which they can expect to exercise a determining influence on events. M. Thiers, in the course of nature, has gone to his rest; Alexander the emancipator has been removed by a violent death; but the great German ruler still survives, seventeen years from the time when M. Thiers was counting upon his great age as an element of hope for France. Nevertheless the soundness of M. Thiers's analysis of the European situation is vindicated by the relation to one another in which the Powers stand to-day. It is on the life of the present Emperor of Germany that the peace of Europe hangs.

It remains to be seen how far M. Thiers's calculation will prove itself true, that the personal antagonism between the present Tzar and the Crown Prince of Germany may be securely relied upon to bring about a Russo-German war. It looks at the present moment as if peace were almost as much imperilled by the uncertainty of his life as by the uncertainty of that of the Emperor. The present Tzar has at least shown clearly enough, in his dealings with Prince Alexander of Battenberg, that such personal considerations profoundly affect his policy. Again, it is at least certain that, anxious as the German statesmen are for permanent peace, if that be possible, it is to the securing of peace during the lifetime of the present Emperor that all their present efforts are directed. A truce dependent on the life of a man of the Emperor's age can scarcely be one of great length, as time is reckoned in the history of nations. It can hardly, therefore, be without interest, even as a question of the immediate future of European policy, to consider the conditions under which the two great empires must engage if they should ever meet in arms. For reasons on the face of facts, on which we shall have occasion to enlarge presently, the matter is one of vital importance to ourselves. We have spoken of the characteristics of both armies already. We propose, therefore, now to consider the nature of the operations which the frontiers of the two Powers will impose upon either army in defence or offence.

I. *The German and Russian frontiers.* — The superiority of the German military frontier on the Russian side is much more obvious than it is on the French. It has been elaborately discussed; and we do not know, at all events, any opinions which have been given, unless it be in some chauvinist Russian newspaper, in favour of the superior advantages of the Russian frontier over the German, so long, that is, as Austria and Germany are in alliance. The importance, however, of the Austro-German frontier to Germany, in the event of a war with Russia, is so great that, if it were on that account alone, it would seem to be a certainty that Germany must fight to save Austria from destruction.[1]

During the last seven years, Russia has certainly

---

[1] The recent publication of the treaty of 1879 does not leave much doubt on this point now. It was hotly contested by Sir C. Dilke.

done rather more than Germany to improve her position on her eastern frontier. She has made Warsaw into a great intrenched camp. She has greatly increased the defences of Ivangorod (or Demblin), of Modlin (or Novo-Georgievisk), of Goniondz (Sperfort), of Kovno, and of Lutzk. She has increased the number of her railways running into Poland, and has made lines running towards Kholm and Rovno, which would facilitate the supply of an army on the Austrian frontier. Meantime Germany, beyond completing what she had been engaged upon since 1870, and in addition, what may be looked upon as ordinary fortress repairs, has only perfected her railway system along the Polish frontier, where it was defective before. But nothing has been done on either side substantially to alter the balance of advantage as to the frontiers which existed in 1879. At the end of that year, two papers, giving each an elaborate study of the military frontiers of the two countries, were published, one by a German officer, under the title of 'Die Befestigung und Vertheidigung der Deutsch-Russichen Grenze der Deutschen Armee dargestellt von einem Deutschen Offizier'[1] (The Fortification and Defence of

[1] Of which a new edition has been published this year. We refer in the text to these only, because they are probably the most accessible and most complete statements of the facts. The number of articles that have appeared on the subject is legion. A very elaborate and careful study of the Polish theatre of war, 'Skizzen

the Russo-German Frontier, reviewed for the benefit of the German Army, by a German Officer) —and another by an Austrian officer, Captain Kirchhammer, 'Deutschlands Nordost - Grenze' (The North-Eastern Frontier of Germany). The substance of both of them was translated in 1880 by Sir Lumley Graham, and appears in the Journal of the United Service Institution, vol. xxiv. Any one who desires to make a fuller study of the subject, and to understand in detail the grounds we have for the opinions we expressed in our first article as to the superior strength of the German frontier, cannot do better than refer to that paper. The substantial facts of the case have not been changed in any material degree, except as to the section on Russian fortifications, which requires the modifications we have given, and except, further, that a certain number of the Russian lines which were then single have been

aus dem europaischen Russland,' has been published by Captain Janki, professor at the Metz War School. It is, however, too full of detail for general readers. Among periodical papers, two interesting articles appeared in the 'Augsburg Gazette,' 21st and 22d March 1882, and another in the 'Golos,' 8th November 1880. A scheme of invasion of Russia by "Sarmaticus," and a review of this in the 'Novoe Vremia' of April 1886, are among the most recent. We have been indebted to Captain A'Court of the Rifle Brigade, who has been for a long time a careful student of the Russian army, for drawing our attention to these. The most valuable study of the Austro-Russian frontier was that of the late General Haymerlé. Marga's study, to which Sir C. Dilke refers, seems to have been based on Haymerlé's lectures.

doubled. The discussion is so sound and able that it would not be easy to improve upon it. Naturally the Austrian officer is rather more anxious than the German to insist on the importance to Germany of the alliance of Austria; but the German admits this also, and there can be very little question that substantially Captain Kirchhammer's views are correct.

We should observe, to begin with, that the Russian railways which have been added since 1880, as well as the old ones, are very different from the German lines. If as many as four trains travel over the most important lines in the day, it represents their full number. Bradshaw does not acknowledge some of the smaller lines, and gives only two trains a-day for others. Curiously enough, for a country like Russia, few of the railways belong to the Government. Altogether, the staff that is kept up on them is in no way adapted to undertake the charge of great movements of troops by rail, and their entraining and detraining arrangements are naturally on a scale proportioned to their normal wants. Railways under these circumstances are amazingly slow in the despatch of great numbers of men. On the other hand, it must be recognised that Russia maintains permanently during peace an enormous body of troops in Poland at all times. Her doing so, however, seems to suggest that she has some fear lest, if she did not sit pretty heavily on the supposed corpse of poor Poland, it might give signs of having been prematurely buried. For our own part, we are disposed to believe, with Sir Charles Dilke, that no great Polish forces will ever again fight in arms against Russia. Nevertheless, those who most nearly watch the ancient kingdom are convinced that a hostile army would find within it a population by no means so patriotically disposed to resist attack upon Russia, as, let us say, the inhabitants of Moscow. If Warsaw is ever set on fire to expel an army engaged in the invasion of Russia, the fire will not have been ignited by the citizens.

A very interesting paper, by Karl Blind, which appeared in the 'Fortnightly Review' for August, offers striking evidence against the current theory to which Sir Charles Dilke has given his support, that the anti-Russian element in Poland is purely that of a small aristocratic class. It would be scarcely possible to have evidence which throws more light from within the revolutionary circles on a very obscure part of history. Karl Blind distinctly alleges that the last Polish revolt was essentially a popular one. He further shows that the agrarian arrangements, which are assumed by Sir Charles Dilke to have made revolt against Russia for the future impossible, were, in fact, initiated by the National Junta, were at first opposed by Russia, and were only accepted by her as ultimately inevitable. If the popular memory of these facts is as vivid as popular tradition is apt to be, they are an element that must not be ignored in the political balance of Eastern Europe. Furthermore, Karl Blind offers some evidence to show that even in 1864 the Poles themselves recognised that Prussian Poland had become essentially German. Prussia has no longer any interest in checking Polish discontent against Russia.

These considerations are of importance, because, throughout almost its entire length, the frontier of Russia, which marches with that of Germany, is the frontier of Poland. In all discussions on the invasion of Russia by Germany, it is assumed that Poland will be the object of German attack. In the discussion of Russian invasion of Germany, in addition to that of advance from Poland, there is another possible line, the existence of which is of great importance to England, because it shows how, in the event of actual war between the two great empires, England might afford the most material assistance to Germany. We do not think that our military judgment is affected by this fact; but it has always seemed to us that the line of invasion which would be most advantageous for Russia would be that across the Niemen, and by the line of the Baltic. For, as the "German officer" says, "the Russian fleet would completely command the sea, and would have access to numerous good harbours."

The powerful defences which have been erected by Prussia in the extreme north angle of the kingdom along the Baltic, would be very difficult to take by a Russian army which was not supported by a fleet having complete command of the sea. For the works of Memel, Pillau, and Königsberg, together with the two arms of the sea known as "Haffs," and the rivers which run into them, form together one vast fortress of which Königsberg is the key. Königsberg cannot be invested till the invader has forced the entrance of the "Frisches Haff," which enables Königsberg to maintain communication with Danzig. Supported by a powerful fleet, the advance could ultimately be made. So advancing, a Russian army would be striking straight for the line of communications of any German army that should attempt to invade Poland. It would be directly covering its own communications, and could fall back at once if menaced by superior force. Nevertheless, even by this line the difficulties that it would have to encounter in the fortresses we have named, and in Danzig, Graudenz, and Thorn, on the line of the Vistula, are sufficiently serious.

We have spoken first of this line because it is to some extent external to the question of attack against or from Poland, which would, we believe we may say with certainty, be the direction taken by any German invasion of Russia.

The general form of the frontier of Poland "at

first sight would appear to give Russia great offensive power." We purposely quote these words from Sir Lumley Graham, because we cannot help believing that they exactly represent the semblance of advantage which has, in our judgment, deceived Sir Charles Dilke as to the relative power for offence and defence represented by the two frontiers. We can hardly put the matter better than Sir Lumley has done in these words: "No one can look at the map of Europe without being struck by the extraordinary configuration of the Russo-German frontier, which is identical with that established in 1815 between Prussia and Russia, and the outline of which was determined by historical rather than by geographical considerations. The old kingdom of Poland, which has since 1815 formed part of the dominions of the Czar, is driven like a huge wedge (200 miles in thickness) into the body of Germany within 200 miles of its heart (Berlin); whilst the advanced provinces of Germany enfold Russian Poland like two mighty arms: the left and longer one (East Prussia) extending some 200 miles; the right one (Silesia) some 70 miles behind its foremost point, the latter arm being prolonged for a further distance of nearly 200 miles by the Austrian province of Galicia. The extremity of Germany's longer arm is, however, not less than 500 or 600 miles from the heart of Russia, whether you consider that heart to be St Petersburg or Moscow."

But long before "Prussia" had become "Germany," her statesmen had fully realised the danger which thus existed for them. Humble as Prussia was to Russia, her deliverer, for many years subsequent to 1815, she steadily pursued the course of securing her frontier by every means which art could devise. Of late years her plans have been carried out so systematically that it is not surprising that since 1880 she has rested content with things as they were, only completing characteristically enough her railway system.

For essentially, as on her western so on her eastern frontier, it is on the threefold power of rapid mobilisation, of rapid and perfect railway transport, and of fortresses which would enable her active army in the field to manœuvre in every direction with advantage, that she depends. As against France so against Russia, she possesses the advantages of a natural frontier so fortified by art that her army can at pleasure rapidly develop its force for striking into the heart of the enemy's country, or can fall back upon a powerful river of which she commands all the passages, with the option of holding or destroying those she pleases. As against France so against Russia, her striking offensive point is pushed far out beyond the great defensive fortress river-line.

To make clear the nature of these positions, let us now go rather more into detail. The province of East Prussia, which is wedged in between Poland and the Baltic, is covered all along its southern frontier, which faces Poland, by a series of lakes and marshes. Movement is here, as in Poland, much restricted by the nature of the country, which makes transport very difficult, except by the best roads. The two great highways are held by Germany at Lötzen and Osterode; though, acting on the same principle as she has adopted on her French frontier, she no longer maintains Osterode as a fortress. Thorn on the Vistula, just inside the Prussian frontier, was, by works completed in 1880, made into a great intrenched camp, with five great forts on the right bank and three on the left. Thorn commands not only the Vistula, but its tributary the Drewenz, which runs from the lakes to fall into the Vistula just south of Thorn. The Drewenz forms for a considerable distance the frontier line. Behind all this frontier, Prussia has now a complete railway line covered by the Drewenz, the fortresses, and the lakes. Four great railways converge on Thorn, giving communication with the interior of Germany, forward along the frontier into East Prussia, south-westward around the western frontier of Poland, and northward behind the Vistula. Thorn also covers one of the only four Russian railways which meet the German lines. Only one Russian railway crosses the Vistula at Warsaw; one branch along the right bank crosses the German frontier near Mlava, one, after the crossing, towards Thorn, while the third runs completely south towards Myslovitz, at the extreme south point of the common Polish and German frontier. The fourth line over the frontier is that from Goniondz to Lötzen. On the other hand, Germany has complete communication from the interior to that part of the Vistula which forms the border line of the province of East Prussia, and her railways pass thence into the province from Graudenz and Marienburg, two fortified bridge-heads, while Thorn and Danzig are the great fortress barriers which secure it on right and left.

Looking now along the frontier south-westwards from Thorn. Posen on the Wartha has been converted since 1870 into a great intrenched camp of the first class, with eleven detached forts. It is about forty miles from the point of the Russian frontier which juts farthest into Germany. Six lines of railway unite here. Next to Posen lies Glogau, a strong bridge-head on the Oder. These form the advanced German fortresses towards Russia. Behind them lies Küstrin, commanding the junction of the Oder and the Netze, the favourite type of site for a great German fortress, because an enemy cannot invest such a one without dividing his army into three sections, each liable to separate attack.

The whole of the country to the south of Thorn, Posen, and Küstrin is interlaced with very numerous railways, which would permit the transfer of Prussian forces in any direction along the frontier; but as a direct advance eastwards upon Poland would never, for reasons we shall presently note, be the most favourable direction for German attack, hardly any of these railways have been led up to the frontier line.

Let us now look across the border at the condition of Poland itself. The peculiarity of the ground lies in this, that it is a vast plain, cut off from the great mass of Russia by the enormous Pinsk Marshes. Of the defence of the kingdom, and of its general military power, Warsaw is the centre. Unquestionably, the recent adaptation to modern war of the Warsaw works, and the fortifications of Novo-Georgievisk, have added greatly to the merely defensive strength of this base. The position at Ivangorod makes the whole of this line of the Russian Vistula strong, so far as the completeness of the fortresses is concerned; but the defect of the base as such is well expressed by the "German officer" when, after speaking of a number of Russian railway projects, which, though their proposal was already of old standing seven years ago, have not been carried out, he adds: "All these additions, however, will be of little effect from a military point of view upon the utility of the railways west of the Vistula, as long as the passage of this river, and consequently the connection of the railways on its left bank with those from the interior of Russia, is only to be effected by the one bridge at Warsaw. It will be absolutely necessary to build several railway bridges over the river before you can calculate upon concentrating a Russian army on the central and southern portions of the German frontier with the speed demanded by the present style of making war." [1]

Now, no fresh bridges have been constructed over the Russian part of the Vistula, and the want of manœuvring facility which this implies, marks the typical difference between the Russian power and the German. Furthermore, a direct advance upon Germany westwards would be necessary to take advantage of the position which, from the point of view of what Sir Charles Dilke rather happily calls "map-makers' war," looks so valuable for Russia. Of course, if mere distance on a map determined military movements, the thrusting forward of Poland into the heart of Germany ought to give Russia a great opportunity for attack. Direct advance from Warsaw westwards is, however, prohibited by the fact that there are no rail-

[1] Journal of the United Service Institution, vol. xxiv. p. 137.

K

ways in that part of Poland to facilitate supply. Furthermore, the country is so difficult to traverse, that the army that began the march would have dwindled into very different numbers before it had accomplished it. Finally, from East Prussia Germany could, from an amply supplied base, aided by every kind of railway facility, strike across the communications of the invader.

It is rather significant that even the " German officer," though he naturally does not enlarge on the subject, assumes as a *sine quâ non* the friendship of Austria, which he regards as an absolute datum. That granted, any attack from the Russian base on the Vistula, passing to the south of Silesia, which must in any case be very eccentric, would be impossible till Austria was conquered. Undoubtedly, on the other hand, with Austria at the feet of Russia, invasion of the southern portion of Silesia would be relatively easy; simply because Prussia, knowing the practical impossibility of direct invasion westwards from Poland, has no fortified place in this district south of Glogau, itself little more than a strong bridge-head. Neisse and Glatz, her two southward fortresses, would be completely out of the line of advance.

Hence Russian attack from Poland is virtually limited either to a movement upon East Prussia directly northward, which would encounter all the difficulties of the line of the lakes, and be met by a far more rapid German concentration; or along the line of the Vistula, which would have the advantage of that stream for a highway, and be to a large extent assisted by two of the lines of railway which run towards the frontier.

But it is as against this movement along the Vistula that the German defences are strongest. The advance along the right bank would meet the defences of the Prussian Vistula. Against the movement by the left bank, between Thorn and Posen, a distance of 80 miles, there spread at intervals great swampy forests, which would impede movement and restrict the invader very closely to the neighbourhood of the fortresses themselves; while the facilities in rear for Prussian concentration and action are ample—and here, as always, the counterstroke from East Prussia would be an element of danger. The "German officer," rather cynically we think, suggests for Russia a double movement—part along the Vistula from Poland, on either the right or left bank, and part by the line we have already referred to as what seems to us the best, that altogether independent of Poland, moving upon Königsberg and the north from the great Russian depot of Dünaburg and from Vilna. Such an attempt to move in two separate columns, unless each column was in overwhelming force, which, from the nature of the country, would not be easy, must give opportunities to a German general for dealing blows right and left against either army while separated by the lake region of East Prussia. Thus an attack by Russia upon Germany appears to be one which offers every kind of advantage to the Germans, either for a prolonged resistance with inferior forces, or if in approximately equal numbers, for striking deadly blows against the invader.

Unquestionably the character of the Polish region and the neighbouring provinces is of a kind that offers also many facilities for pure defensive action to Russia. But it presents none of those combinations which give to the defender the opportunity for counterstrokes against an invader which the German frontier supplies. The province is dependent upon its artificial communications by railway with Russia for any rapid reinforcement, because of the difficult country which separates it from the interior. As Captain Kirchhammer says: "The value of these communications as a whole is much weakened by the fact that the two northernmost lines are much exposed in consequence of their situation in close vicinity to the German frontier. The Russian base is certainly not well adapted to military requirements. First of all, it is too narrow in proportion to the extent of the German theatre of war; moreover, it is outflanked from the very first; in a word, it is weak."

In rear of the main defensive line of the Russian Vistula stands the very important fortress of Brest Litewsk, which protects the connection of a vast number of railways, and is on the Bug, about 110 miles east of Warsaw. It is intended to cover the concentration of the Russian forces coming from the various quarters of the empire, whose movements are separated by the great Pinsk Marshes. It seems, however, to us that it would be almost as difficult a task for the Russians to protect from Prussian cavalry the lines of railway which connect Brest Litewsk with Warsaw, as it would be difficult for the Russian cavalry to disturb any of the railway lines which are needed for the German concentration. This is the more remarkable, because the Prussian railways run much more conveniently near to the frontier than the Russian.

So far as the immediate attack of Germany upon Russia is concerned there are no other fortresses that need be taken into account. For of all countries in the world Russia is the last which can safely be attacked by plunging into the depths of "her large and almost impenetrable stretches of marsh and of forest imperfectly supplied with roads."

"Germany must," as the German officer puts it, "while standing on the defensive, on the eastern frontier of East Prussia, at once take possession of such a large portion of Poland as to cripple the action of Russia on that side."

"The kingdom of Poland is the most densely populated portion of the Russian empire, and is well adapted, from the nature of the country, for operations on a large scale.[1] The task, therefore, which would devolve upon a German commander would not be impossible; and its successful completion, entailing as it would a prolonged occupation of the conquered country, might well lead to the attainment of the object of the war. Otherwise it would remain for the German leader to proceed with his further operations according to circumstances, his chances of success being much increased in every way by the preliminary occupation of Poland."[2]

For this purpose, in a war in which Germany could afford to employ her troops in an attack upon Russia, without troubling herself about another enemy, it seems to us that, from the nature of the Russian communications with Poland, Germany ought almost with certainty to be able, for a time, to isolate the force in Poland before it could receive material reinforcements. That force is undoubtedly large, probably more than twice as large as the army which Germany has in the neighbouring provinces ready to bring against it.

---

[1] An expression which, we must admit, seems to us not to take adequate account of Napoleon's great enemy, the Polish mud. Still he certainly did conduct there operations on a large scale.

[2] Journal of the United Service Institution, vol. xxiv. p. 145.

But the conditions of the frontier would make it impossible for it to act against Germany before her mobilisation was complete. Any premature advance westward or northward would only tend to separate it more from the main Russian army, and to expose its communications more completely to the enemy. Moreover, Russia has taken a precaution which, while it certainly indicates that she is more afraid of attack herself than hopeful of a rapid success from sudden invasion of her neighbours, would seriously interfere with her throwing her Polish army so quickly across the frontier as to interfere with mobilisation. She has taken as the gauge of her railways 5 feet instead of 4 feet 8½ inches, which is the common gauge of Germany, Austria, and the Continent generally. Both she and her neighbours have shifting axles provided to overcome the difficulty, but the extent to which they would practically facilitate transport is very uncertain, and they are likely to be better managed by German than by Russian railway engineers. Therefore, under such conditions, the contest would not and could not be between the army of occupation of Poland and the German peace army. It would be the mobilised German army which would be able to throw itself upon the army in Poland. If that takes place, we are of the opinion of Captain Kirchhammer, that "the overlapping form of the German base will make any line of operations, having for its objective Russian Poland, strategically safe, and will give the commander-in-chief considerable facilities, should he wish to change that line.

"The want of cohesion between Poland and the remainder of the Russian empire will naturally suggest to the German general the idea of slipping in between the two, of completely isolating the regions of the Vistula, of overwhelming its garrison, and of preventing the arrival of reinforcements from the interior.

"Whether the main German operation should be directed from Posen-Thorn against the triangle Warsaw, Novo-Georgievisk, Serotsk, or from Königsberg-Lötzen against Brest-Litewsk—whether to play a safe or a bold game—whether to aim at the Russian army or at its communications,—he who has to decide this question must go beyond mere geographical considerations; he must take account of a great mass of circumstances, and above all he must reckon up the armed force which Germany can hurl on Russia. Our rapid survey satisfies us that the north-eastern frontier of Germany forms an excellent base both for offence and defence.

"The strategist will find in it almost an ideal theatre of war, a field for numerous and varied combinations."[1]

An almost similar result would occur if Poland

---

[1] Journal of the United Service Institution, vol. xxiv. p. 148.

had been so far denuded of troops by the consequences of war elsewhere as to leave to a portion of the German army the opportunity of striking against it, though the main body of the German forces were otherwise engaged.

We mention these several cases because it is highly improbable, in the present condition of European politics, that a war will ever take place in which Germany and Russia will be engaged against one another without allies on either hand. Not only the Prussian frontier but the heart of the German Empire would be open to an attack directed from Russia in possession of a secured hold upon Galicia. This fact, and the isolation in which Germany would be left if Austria was crushed, make it scarcely possible to conceive that Austria will be allowed to be seriously defeated before Germany takes the field. We cannot believe, as Sir Charles Dilke thinks, that Russia would be allowed to wrench Galicia from Austria. Similarly, the very existence of Austria depends on the support of Germany. For though we do not believe that Austrian force is *une quantité négligible*, we certainly do not think that, taken alone, she is equal in power to Russia; and she knows well that, in the long-run, no terms that she can make will prevent Russia from feeling her to be an obstacle in her path, while one most powerful section of her people will resent all terms made with Russia. On the other hand, it needs no prophet to predict that "the Chassepots," or rather now the Lebels, "will go off of themselves," if ever Germany is at war with Russia.

II. *Austria.*—Here, therefore, it becomes important to consider what contribution Austria can at present offer to the resistance to Russian aggression. The sketch which Sir Charles Dilke has given of the present weakness of Austria appears to us to be defective in this, that while most that he has said is true as a bare statement of fact, it ignores all the elements which compensate this weakness, and it does not take account of the special character which Austrian resistance to Russia would assume. There is no story in the history of the world more remarkable than that of Austria. It is the history of the triumph of diplomacy over war, and yet of a diplomacy dependent always for its power on a certain kind of military strength. To us it seems that though undoubtedly the heterogeneous character of the monarchy, which has always weakened its armies, is more apparent on the surface than ever, yet that, in a contest with Russia which should take place a year or two hence, Austria would be practically stronger than she has been at any time in her history. The Austrian armies have probably sustained more defeats than any other troops in Europe, yet over and over again she has become the decisive Power, whose influence, thrown into the scale, has determined the issue of victorious war. It was her union with the Allies that proved fatal to Napoleon in 1813. Her union with us during the campaigns of Marlborough is connected with some of the most glorious periods of our own military history. The power of recuperation which she has again and again shown after defeat has been marvellous. It is no doubt due to the fact that her population, almost entirely agricultural, has always furnished a vast supply of hardy healthy soldiers; while the masses of her rural folk have, despite the socialism of the towns, been less disposed towards revolutionary changes than any others in Europe.[1] Patriotism, except in Hungary, is no doubt difficult for the inhabitants of the agglomerate empire. It is hard to know towards what nation their patriotism should be felt. Nevertheless the loyalty of many races—the Tyrolese, for instance—and generally a certain attachment to the Royal house, if it does not supply all the motive power which armies need, saves Austria from many of the risks which some of her neighbours run. It is of no small consequence that all the heterogeneous population feels the Emperor's

---

[1] The tremendous shock which she sustained in 1848 was far more due to a conflict of races than to any insurrectionary tendencies among the masses of the people.

authority to be essential to them. Certainly those who have most recently been studying the people of Austria are not disposed to think that Russian propagandism has made any way even in Bohemia or among the Slave populations. No doubt it is true, as Sir Charles Dilke says, that the difficulties of such an empire are aggravated by the adoption of popular forms of government which tend to give play to jealousies within the empire. But on the other hand, it is well to remember that as long ago at least as the campaign of Blenheim, the weakness of Austria against which her enemies directed their efforts, was the hostility of the most warlike section of her people to the Imperial Government. It was precisely in order to give scope to the possible effects of Hungarian insurrection that Louis XIV. planned the scheme of war which was defeated by Marlborough's famous march, of which the great purpose was to save the empire from destruction. Prussia hoped to secure the same advantage in 1866. To-day, amid all the efforts which have been put forth by Austria to prepare for the coming fray, those who have most enthusiastically responded to the call have been the Hungarian subjects of the Kaiser. The enthusiasm which in Hungary has greeted new arrangements of the Landsturm, which have vastly added to the numerical forces at the disposal of the Austrian generals, led to officers and men of the army, and to members of the Hungarian Parliament, patiently submitting last year to the drudgery of special military courses, designed for developing the warlike power of a race apt beyond most others in the art. The change which is thus represented, cannot fail to show itself in fighting efficiency. Never before has Austria entered upon war, with Hungarians passionately enlisted on her side, without Italian regiments ready to lay down the arms of a hated service the moment an opportunity presented itself. Tyrolese and German loyalty is not less than of old.

Of the fourteen chief races which are included in the Austrian monarchy, it appears to us that a war against Russia will unite at least twelve in more enthusiasm for the cause than has ever been felt in an Austrian struggle before. Only two, the Serbs and the Ruthenians, are both Slaves and of the Greek Church. It is tolerably certain that the bitter persecution of alien religions in Russia will have estranged, among several of the other Slave races, such as the Czechs and Croats, any sympathies which race affinities or Slave propagandism may have produced; while, on all accounts, German, Jew, Magyar, Saxon, and Italian have their own special and bitter feud with the Tzar. Therefore, so far as it is possible to judge of such matters by any other test than that of trial, the inner moral weakness which has always hitherto made the magnificent presentments on parade of the Austrian armies a deceptive indication of their strength, seems at least likely to have disappeared. No doubt the discrepancies of language will remain a difficulty; but that is, as compared with the other, a secondary matter.[1] It is not a little remarkable that one of the earliest protests against the Metternich system in 1848, came from the army, in the form of a pamphlet by an officer, Karl Möring, entitled 'Die Sibyllinische Bücher,' in which, declaring that "the Austrian has no fatherland," he pointed out the increased power which would be given to Austria if a more liberal system were introduced. For a very interesting account of this incident and its effect, as well as of the several races of the Austrian empire, in tabular form with their religions, and for another matter which we shall next mention, we may refer our readers to a volume just published on 'The Revolutionary Movement of 1848-49 in Italy, Austria-Hungary, and Germany.'[2] The same author brings out a fact which is of no little importance to our present purpose. It ap-

---

[1] Only, however, "as compared with the other," I am far from underrating its vast importance.

[2] By C. Edmund Maurice. London: George Bell & Sons, York Street, Covent Garden, 1887. Marga gives a more complete account of the races, but it is not so easily seen at a glance. Oddly enough, the Jews, who number, according to Marga, 1,400,000, are omitted from the book we have referred to in the text.

pears that the Bohemian historian Palacky was asked to join the Revolutionary Assembly at Frankfort as representative of Bohemia. He, speaking in the name of his countrymen, protested against their being called upon to send such representatives at all, on two grounds: one, the necessity of an independent Austria as a barrier against Russia; the other, the fact that "Austria, which must necessarily remain an empire, could not consent to a close union with" a republican "Germany without breaking to pieces." We venture to commend this statement from a brother historian, who may be supposed to know something of the several races of the empire in which he lived, to Mr Freeman, *apropos* to his letters to the 'Times' of September 17th and October 15th, 1887.

It has not been from lack of producing great generals, skilled officers, a perfect discipline, or hardy soldiers, that Austria has so often failed. Wallenstein, Prince Eugene, the Archdukes Charles and Albert, have been leaders of the highest class. But again and again in the past, Court intrigue has kept the genius from command, and left to the pedant or the *beau sabreur* the opportunity to destroy armies that in better hands might have given a different account of their enemies. Both Court intrigue and the exclusiveness of aristocratic privilege are likely to play a much less dangerous part in the future than they have done in the past of Austrian history. No doubt it is true, as Mr Freeman says in the letters to which we have referred, that the Croatians and others of the various peoples ruled over by the Hapsburgs are conscious of claims which have been by no means dealt with in the Austro-Hungarian compact. But, so far as we have been able to ascertain from those who have most recently studied the feeling of these nationalities, they are conscious of the danger of allowing the empire to become a loose bundle of sticks such as Mr Freeman would desire it to be. They cherish, no doubt, certain sentimental grievances; but these are by no means at present likely seriously to affect the zeal of men in the ranks.

Meantime the efforts that have been recently made towards developing the numbers and improving the fighting efficiency of the army have been vigorous. It is not easy to ascertain how far the fortresses have been completed. Austria is always in financial difficulties, and fortresses of the modern type are costly luxuries. Cracow (or Krakem) and Przemysl, Olmutz, Komorn, and Pola[1] in Dalmatia, have all lately been receiving attention, as well as, for southern war, Mostar[1] in the Herzegovina. It is impossible to say how much may be done, before a war, to render them

[1] Both Mostar and Pola are beyond the limits of our frontier map.

fit for use under modern conditions, as the works, so far as Austria is able to afford the expense, are now in progress. It is certainly not a little remarkable that Austria, which secured her hold in Italy by one of the most powerful combinations of fortresses ever devised, has never succeeded in completing her defence system as worked out by her own engineers. There is no story to tell of carefully planned artificial improvements of the natural frontier such as we have given for Prussia. On the other hand, few countries have a more commanding situation naturally than Austria possesses towards Russia. The great range of the Carpathians forms for her a kind of natural citadel of which Galicia is the glacis. From them she can strike northward into Poland even more easily than Germany can strike south; while her position as against any Russian movement to the south of her empire is so commanding that Russia has never yet ventured to attack Turkey without coming to an understanding with her. As against attack, she has the enormous advantage that the Russian troops, which are now said to be collecting in Poland and the south, could not attack her from these quarters without giving her the opportunity of dealing with each of them separately. Any movement of the Russians from Poland, as long as Austria and Germany are in alliance, is seriously affected by the difficulties of passage across the directly western frontier of Poland, which we have described. She must, to attack either Power, move north or south, and therefore expose herself to the risk of attack from the one which is not immediately assailed.

According to a French officer, who has, in the columns of the 'Revue Militaire de l'Étranger,' been devoting nearly a year to a statement of the present organisation of the Austrian army, the results of which were summed up in the issue for August 30th last, the total infantry of the Imperial Hapsburg army, including standing army, Landwehr, and Landsturm, but excluding depots of recruits and untrained men, is now 32,600 officers and 1,380,000 men, the cavalry 3358 officers and 88,263 men. They have also been increasing the *personnel* of their artillery by some 28,000 men. Probably, therefore, including artillery, the numbers may be reckoned at something considerably exceeding a million and a half. For a population of 39 millions odd that is certainly not as formidable a result as either France or Germany has produced; but, thanks to the recent political action of Russia, very considerable armies may now be reckoned as added to those which Austria would employ, if the quarrel arose about Russian interference with Bulgaria. It is hardly too much to say that Bulgaria, Roumania, and Servia might all in that case be reckoned on to give any support they could to Austria. The Roumanians showed their efficiency in 1876 by saving the Russians from ignominious disaster, and were rewarded with a treachery which they have not forgotten. The Bulgarians have also shown that they could fight, and the support of a large disciplined army would probably make valuable troops of them all. Together, it is believed at present that they could put eight army-corps, or say 240,000 men, into the field, without counting their troops of second line, the organisation of which is by no means complete.

The Austrian army, as organised for war, would be probably raised to forty-nine divisions of 18,000 each, by help of the new organisation. The discrepancy between these figures and those which are represented by the million and a half of trained men whom we have mentioned above, exists in all the armies, whether of Russia, Germany, or France, in greater or less degree. Thus, out of the German total of two millions, 1,265,746 constitute the field-army; and of the 2,721,000 of the French, 1,211,000 constitute the field-army.[1] An addition to the 882,000, composing the forty-nine Austrian divi-

[1] The whole character of the French organisation has, however, been recently changed. By a law introduced on June 25, 1887, by General Ferron, forty-five battalions have been added to the forces actually with the colours. This has been gained by a sacrifice of all available cadres to such an extent that French critics themselves believe that the mobilisation of all but the first line will be reduced to hopeless confusion. The law took effect from October 1, 1887. It is hardly possible as yet to estimate what the result may be.

sions, of the 240,000 men of the three minor states, would raise the Austrian field-army, which compares with these, to about 1,120,000 men.

It is impossible to estimate what proportion of the Russian nominal grand total of seven millions could actually be moved to attack Austria; but considering the enormous extent of her almost roadless territory, and the proportion which has always hitherto existed between the paper numbers of the Russian army and the force it was possible to place in the field, there does not seem to us any reason to believe that the forces which she would actually deliver in the area of war would be practically greater than those which Austria and the minor states would be able to maintain in action. On one side and on the other it will become a question of the numbers that can be fed and supplied with ammunition. That, though it is in part a question of money, is by no means altogether so. The numbers that could be supplied from Germany and fed in France afford no means of judging what would be possible for armies dependent upon such railways as Russia possesses. Moreover, the railway connection across the border between Russia and Austria is even more slender than it is between Russia and Germany. Already there are clear indications that the Russians are finding it impossible to provide for their nominal army sufficient numbers of non-commissioned or commissioned officers of even such quality as have hitherto supplied her forces. At this moment the Russian infantry has probably the best breech-loader possessed by any army; but by the end of 1888, the Austrian infantry is to be armed throughout with magazine rifles. It may or may not be the case that in all respects magazine rifles are a great improvement on effective breech-loaders for fighting purposes. What is certain is that the army which does not possess them, and finds itself in the presence of those that do, will be at a great disadvantage as to the *morale* of the troops.

We have already in a former article given so fully our reasons for distrusting the effect upon the efficiency of the Russian cavalry of the changes which the present Tzar has introduced, that the value of our estimate of the Austrian cavalry must depend on the soundness of that statement, based as it was on authorities taken from every country in Europe. If that contention be right, then we have no hesitation in saying that the Austrian cavalry is second to none in Europe. The Austrian artillery has unfortunately been the subject of so many experiments and failures that we confess we are entirely unable to judge of the power it would actually show in war. So far as peace manœuvres furnish means of judging, it is in a high state of efficiency.

In discussing the position in which Austria

stands to Russia, Sir Charles Dilke has evidently misunderstood Captain Marga. He says: "As a great foreign military writer, Marga, has consolingly observed of Austria-Hungary, in that which is the first of all the military works of the day, 'After several defeats she can retire into the wooded Carpathians;' but he adds, 'The road to Vienna is thus uncovered.'"[1] But Marga, p. 142, vol. ii., says this, not in the least in order to show that the Austrian army is likely to be defeated, but in order to defend a proposition that Austria has a much more effective defence against one particular line of Russian attack than that of retiring by the line of the Carpathians. "C'est en s'appuyant sur les principaux cours d'eau, ainsi que sur les places de Cracovie et de Przemysl, que l'Autriche chercherait à couvrir la Galicie," is the previous sentence. Then he shows that for an Austrian army to fall back on the Carpathians in case of defeat would have the disadvantage of uncovering Vienna, and probably of allowing the Russians to break her army in two. This, however, is only to lead up to the argument that, by falling back instead on the San, the Wysloka, and the Donajec, whilst guarding the carriage-roads across the mountains by field fortifications, the Austrian army would completely cover both Vienna and Pesth, and oblige the Russian army to follow its excentric move-

---

[1] The Present Position of European Politics, p. 189.

ment. He had already shown that Russian attack by the left of the Vistula, and so on Cracow, would expose the Russian army to the danger of being cut off from Russia by an Austrian army acting along the right bank. The discussion throughout tends to give the advantage to Austria because of the formidable Pinsk Marshes, which tell more in favour of Austrian than even of German action. But there is a yet more telling sentence of Marga's, saying that, in order to carry out a march on Vienna, Russia "must be very sure of the neutrality of Germany." Sir Charles thinks he has disposed of this awkward phrase, which he does not quote, by adding, "Neither can Germany be trusted to defend Vienna by menacing the long line of the Russian advance; because when Germany ceases to be neutral, the neutrality of France in turn will cease, and Germany will have enough to do to defend the Rhine."[1] Is that so? That is just what we propose to consider next. We may, however, observe in passing, that the number of troops is not very great that are required to cause the collapse of an army which has committed itself to a long line of advance, open to attack throughout its length by fresh forces acting at right angles to it. Russia learnt that both in Asia and in Europe in 1878. It seems hardly conceivable that Sir Charles Dilke will lull her into re-

[1] The Present Position of European Politics, p. 189.

peating, by a march on Vienna exposed to the possible attacks of a hostile Germany, even though engaged against France, the mistakes of the march on the Balkans and the march on Erzeroum. We may safely assume that Bayazid and Plevna are names too deeply burnt into Russian souls for that. If that is so, Sir Charles Dilke's whole theory of the political balance, with Austria *forced* to rest on Italy, tumbles like a house of cards touched at its base.

III. *The position of Germany in a war with both Russia and France combined.*—We now propose to consider the circumstances of vantage and of disadvantage which the two frontiers of Germany and of her neighbours, and the nature of her whole defensive and offensive strength, present to an alliance against her of France and of Russia. That she would stand alone, we disbelieve; that it is in our interest, or in that of Europe, that she and Austria should together stand alone against Russia and France, it will be one of the special purposes of our next article to deny. But it is important to realise what the forces will be that will be brought into the issue by the Power against whom the Franco-Russian alliance, if it ever becomes a fact, will be in the first instance directed.

Undoubtedly an examination of the German methods of national defence must, we think, leave one impression at least upon any of our readers who have realised them as we have laid them before them. They are pre-eminently bold. On both frontiers alike her most effective defence depends on her power of being able to strike offensive blows at the outset of a campaign. Has she the strength, and dare she attempt, to strike offensive blows on both sides of her great empire, at once against two such adversaries as Russia and France? We answer that it is morally certain that her rulers will be much too wise to carry on two long offensive campaigns at both ends of her empire at the same time. But there are offensive strokes like that which Napoleon attempted against the Anglo-allied and Prussian armies during the Waterloo campaign, which are only intended to knock out of time one assailant before another can come on. It appears to us that the central position of the German Empire, guarded on either frontier by the fortified rivers of the Rhine on one side, and of the Vistula and Oder on the other, with the advanced post of Metz thrust out beyond the mountain-barrier of the Vosges on one side, and the arm of East Prussia stretched out along the kingdom of Poland on the other, offers opportunities to a great strategist that are even more "ideal" than those which Captain Kirchhammer has so described. War nowadays has indeed come to be waged on a colossal scale; but there are possibilities involved in the possession by Germany of a middle position covered with a most perfect and carefully devised railway system, and a telegraph network as complete, which stagger one as to the terrible grandeur of the drama which may be enacted by their means almost under our eyes. In a time far shorter than it took Napoleon to transfer his force from Boulogne to Ulm and Austerlitz, far shorter than it took Marlborough to carry out that magnificent campaign from which Napoleon, in all probability, took the idea which rolled up the map of Europe for ten years, a German army might be nowadays transferred from the Rhine to the Vistula, or from Königsberg to Metz. Under given conditions, such a transfer of men from one side of Europe to the other might be made without any knowledge of the movement reaching either of the hostile armies, until one that had been advancing triumphantly was crushed by the new and overwhelming power suddenly thrown into the field, and till the other had lost the opportunity afforded by the diminution of force. For, though the two frontiers of Germany are specially fitted for offensive action, both are adapted also to afford means to a comparatively inferior force for imposing delay on one very superior. The difficult country of Western Poland, the lakes and the shallow *haffs* of East Prussia, the swampy forests between the Wartha and the upper Vistula, the marshy region of the

Obra in the province of Posen, the Polish mud which bothered Napoleon, the strong defences of Thorn and of Posen, the broad Vistula directly intercepting a Russian march through Prussia, as it does not intercept a Prussian stroke against the Russian communications with Poland, will be inconvenient obstacles for those Russian generals, "who," as the "German officer" has it, "after sharing many a disillusion during the late Russo-Turkish war, may wish to satisfy their ardent thirst for glory at the expense of Germany, but who might possibly find out by experience that it is more difficult to gain their object in a war against that Power than even in one against Turkey." The difficulties of the Vosges, the passage of the Rhine, the siege of Metz or Strasbourg, may delay the picking up of the field-marshal's baton by a French general, even when the flash of guns in Poland had set the Chassepots or the Lebels going off of themselves.

It would, of course, be vain to speculate on which side the blow of the central force would, in such a case, be first struck. If, in order to give Austria breathing-time afterwards, it were thought better to join her in overwhelming the force in Poland, then the French might be allowed to advance into positions in the Vosges, where a stroke delivered from the north at their communications would be easier work than a dash at the fortress-forest of the frontier; or the French might be tempted to raise up foes in their rear by a violation of Swiss or Belgian neutrality. Or to take the other side of the theatre of war,—if the decision were to anticipate the French mobilisation, to strike a blow that might induce the French for some time afterwards to hug their fortresses, Austria might then be left for a time to hold her own as best she might, and the stroke at Poland might be subsequently delivered whilst the Russian forces were employed in the Carpathians, or the advance on Vienna might be made disastrous by an even easier movement upon Galicia. Such speculations are only of value in so far as they suggest the possibilities which are offered by her position to Germany. The decision will of course depend on the circumstances of the hour, largely upon the belief in Berlin as to the efficiency of the French mobilisation and the condition of the Russian forces in Poland, the state of the Austrian army, of other political alliances, the time of year, and the probable nature of the weather. We have, however, we think, said enough to explain why, neither as to her frontiers nor as to her military situation, do we believe that as a power in Europe, Germany, though she has before her a tremendous task, has ceased to be the mightiest empire on the Continent. That she is now an essentially conservative and peaceful nation we firmly believe.

That most assuredly she has no temptation to go to war, and that if her most skilful statesmen can save her from that dire calamity they will do so, we are well convinced. Unfortunately no one who studies the present situation believes any more than Sir Charles Dilke that their success can be more than temporary.

At the present moment there are in the world two "fretful realms"; and it is of vital consequence to us to estimate accurately the forces that exist for keeping them in awe. Of those forces we are convinced that Germany must always be the mighty nucleus. We disbelieve that she is in a position scornfully to reject any alliance for the purpose on whose loyalty she can depend. We are certain that it is contrary to the whole policy of her statesmen to do so. For us the great necessity is to realise that Sir Charles Dilke has earnestly pressed upon us, that, now that our frontier virtually marches with that of Russia in Asia, and that we certainly know that her progress towards India is no accident brought on by over-zealous servants, but part of a deliberately designed plan, all the particulars of which are known, we must face the facts like men, and prepare for the inevitable attack. We differ from him as to the means by which we ought to meet it. But we are sure that we cannot do wrong in pressing home this, that no reply has been made to the challenge given in the 'Quarterly Review' of January 1887, to those who know, to deny that they have had *indisputable* evidence before them that Russian action on India is and has been for years deliberate, designed, carefully planned, and that it is hourly approaching the period of overt action.[1] We cannot think that enough has been done to bring this fact home to our people. With our great enemy the case is different. The whole resources of the State are at the disposal of the Tzar, before whom silently the facts which serve as motives for action can be laid. Year after year a policy can be steadily pursued, the results of which are only obvious to us when they are about to be secured. Sir Charles Dilke has himself admirably exposed the reckless indifference to solemn pledges, the ingenious subterfuges, the false analogies which have been used as cloaks to cover from English eyes the steady purpose with which her march proceeds.

[1] The wording of the passage we refer to deserves to be given: "To those who would fain believe that this rapid advance is the result of accidental circumstances, we would, *with full knowledge of the subject*, reply by challenging any high official, either Liberal or Conservative in either India or England, to say *that he had not had absolute proofs before him* that the Russian advance is *the result of a well-matured design* to dispute our empire in the East."—Article "Constantinople, Russia, and India," Quarterly Review, January 1887. For our own part, we cannot doubt that this was an authorised attempt to draw public attention to this vital truth. Sir C. Dilke obviously is not among the officials referred to; the information was probably obtained subsequently to his leaving office. In any case, he knows nothing of the matter.

Now it is not possible that we should meet that deliberate scheme as long as our people are halting between two opinions as to whether Madame Novikoff and her faithful henchman are not honest friends of England, instead of being, as in fact they are—one consciously, the other blinded by flattery, by gratitude for favours received, and by personal vanity—the agents for throwing dust in the eyes of Englishmen. We are sure that Sir Charles Dilke has done good service in endeavouring to persuade our statesmen that great as were the diplomatic facilities of the days of Castlereagh, those days are in fact for England no more. Our people must know things which in those days were wisely for the national good kept from them. Secrecy has, in war, still overwhelming advantage. We believe, as we have already urged, that it is a very great mistake to discuss in public the precise point at which our blow at Russia should be aimed. Such a public discussion as led to the movement on Sebastopol in 1854, would, in these days of completed railways and telegraphs, bring disaster upon the expedition which attempted the advertised attack. But there are many questions of politics as to which we attempt to carry on the old system of playing their own game against nations which can secretly exert all their power when we cannot develop ours, or maintain a constant policy unless the country at large understands the true facts. We entirely agree with Sir Charles Dilke that "if it were possible to conduct the foreign relations of a democratic country, such as England has now become, with secrecy as well as with firm devotion to a fixed line of conduct, no doubt it would be better to leave the consideration of many questions until they actually arise; but at the present moment we suffer from the disadvantages of both systems. We do not fully discuss foreign relations in advance, and make up our minds as to our best course; we do not even take steps to inform ourselves thoroughly as to the facts; but at the same time we encourage our public men to make rash and hasty statements founded upon imperfect knowledge, and we 'go wild' from time to time in various directions."[1]

It would be very easy for us to show that Sir Charles Dilke has offended against his own canons; that he has misinterpreted the meaning of the surrender to China of the station at Port Hamilton; that he has similarly misinterpreted the meaning of the present Government scheme for adding power to our army. It has been precisely because he has not been behind the scenes in these matters that he is not aware that they have been attempts to secure many of the very objects which he himself most earnestly desires. He has struck

[1] The Present Position of European Politics, p. 285.

wild blows, hitting those who have been steadily working to secure real efficiency. Nevertheless, in so far as he has brought before the country the necessity for not shutting our eyes to undoubted facts, and before our statesmen the necessity for keeping the nation informed of the dangers to be faced, he has rendered a great service.

There are not a few of these dangers which he has ignored. He has, for instance, touched far too lightly on the risk to our trade round the Cape of the French occupation of Diego Suarez, the magnificent harbour to the north of Madagascar, and of the Comoro Islands,[1] which together command the Mozambique Channel. The case is the more curious because he has rightly judged that the Cape route, and not the Suez Canal, must necessarily be that on which we chiefly depend during war-time.

We must confess that we have found it extremely difficult to be sure of the exact impression which he has wished to leave by his statements on many of the subjects he has handled. He certainly appeared to us, as he did to many others of his critics, to wish us to believe that Russia was a Power fully a match by herself for Germany and Austria combined. We by no means have committed ourselves to disputing his assertion that, on the whole, Austria is not so strong a Power, if she stands alone, as Russia. Yet, in the "Conclusion" to his now published volume,

[1] Not mentioned at all.

he appears almost to limit himself to that assertion. We are not aware that that position has been anywhere assailed. He has, however, in no wise modified his views as to the value, under present conditions of war, of the Russian infantry or of the Russian cavalry as newly organised. In our first article we cited from almost every country in Europe high authorities against his opinion. We do not, indeed, know where those authorities are to be found to whom he constantly appeals as decisive. The opinions of those whose names ordinarily carry weight are everywhere against him. It seems to us that, in order to support his statement on this subject, he must have inquired either among those who have not been tried, or among those who have been tried and failed. On other questions, as, for instance, when he appeals against Colonel Malleson to high Indian authorities "whom Colonel Malleson would be the first to respect," there is this difficulty, from his habit of citing without naming men,[1] that he evidently is not aware what a conflict of opinion exists as to the question of the proper defence of India among the highest Indian authorities, nor does he quite realise how very intelligible that conflict is. So far as we have been able to ascertain, among those who, without any circumstances

---

[1] A good deal of this difficulty has been removed in his more recent articles. It will be seen that the mentioning of the names in no way weakens the force of anything I have said here.

which tend to obscure their vision, base their opinion upon pure military grounds, and upon the advantage to England of the course to be pursued, there is no dispute as to the facts which we pressed home in our former article. On the one hand, so far as the fighting on the actual Indian frontier is concerned, the farther we can fight Russia away from her base, and therefore the nearer to our Indian frontier, unless we can strike through Persia from an altogether independent base, the stronger we are. On the other hand, though we cannot safely advance upon Herat from India, it is vitally necessary to us to forbid Russia to possess herself of Herat and the Heri Rud. Therefore it is also vitally necessary for us to put pressure upon Russia elsewhere than at Herat in order to protect Herat.

Undoubtedly, if the Afghans were a united people, who could be trusted to adhere religiously to contracts made by a central Power, advance upon Herat would be a question of their friendship or hostility; but that is just the element on which we cannot count. The Afghans are, in fact, a congeries of fierce tribes, who, no matter what bargains we had made with them beforehand, would be apt to break out in our rear after the first check we received in our front. Therefore, advance far beyond the Indian frontier becomes for us most dangerous. Our position there is strongest when it is strictly defensive.

But all the world over human nature is human nature, and the clearest military vision may be obscured by the temptations of a brilliant campaign. The matter may be plausibly put: "We are all agreed that Russia must be stopped from advancing upon Herat,—why should not the campaign to achieve that end be carried out from India itself?" It is not therefore difficult to guess why some of the highest authorities—whose names Sir Charles has not produced, but of whom we will give Sir Charles the benefit of declaring that, as we know their views, we know also that their names would add much weight to his words—should be tempted, against their better judgment, to persuade themselves of the wisdom of a course which would for England be very dangerous. If the question as to the proper course to be pursued by another country and another army under analogous conditions could be submitted to their unbiassed judgment, we have no doubt at all as to the value of their military opinions. The analogies of military history are now sufficiently numerous, and we say unhesitatingly that they all preach—"Strike by all means. Do not wait to be struck, when you know that your enemy is only waiting for the moment which will be best for him to strike you; but do not strike him at the point where he is strongest and you will be weakest."

Sir Charles Dilke, who has not had the means of knowing what, in England at all events, have been the proposals of "the highest authorities" for some time past, puts forward a series of statements, dogmatically given without support of any kind, to the effect that we cannot attack Russia in Europe. He treats the question as though we had nothing to offer in exchange for those facilities for "getting at her in Europe" for which we unquestionably require the aid of other Powers. What he has not told us is, that the great power which Russia has shown in her Asiatic conquests, is that of gaining strength as she goes forward—of assimilating the tribes she has conquered there, as he shows that she has now assimilated the tribes of the Caucasus. The omission in his calculations which Colonel Malleson pointed out is the central point of the whole question:—

"What, then, I may ask, has become of the survivors of the defeat of Geok Tépé in January 1881? Of the many thousand Turkmans who fought, some thousands at least submitted. What, too, has become of the Turkmans of Merv? The whole of these yielded without striking a blow, and we may be sure that Russia did not slaughter them in cold blood. It cannot be that they have no trained horses. The testimony of many travellers, from Burnes down to Vambéry, proves that there has ever been an abundance of horses among the

Turkman tribes—horses ready to do the work of the desert, hardy, stout-hearted, full of endurance. No ; in those nomadic countries it is safe to assert that history repeats itself. From the earliest days, from Mahmoud of Ghazni down to Nadir Shah, the Turkman cavalry have invariably taken service with the conqueror of their desert homes, more especially when they have realised the fact that that conqueror designs to lead them to pastures rich in booty. As light cavalry they can scarcely be surpassed ; they are accustomed to Eastern warfare ; they make war support war. With such men Russia could ill dispense, and we may be sure that she has not dispensed with them. There are, at this moment, not hundreds, but thousands, of them at the beck and call of Russia."[1]

He has taken no notice of this,[2] except by a casual admission that it is the manifest interest of Russia to absorb Northern Persia, "as Russia alone of European Powers can absorb an Eastern country." He quietly proposes to hand over Herat to Russia, because in the "race for Herat Russia has undoubtedly beaten us," ignoring what Colonel Malleson has unanswerably urged as to the vital importance of our preventing Russia

---

[1] "The Fortnightly Reviewer and Russia"—Blackwood's Magazine, April 1887, p. 576.

[2] See the answer to Colonel Malleson, pp. 329, 330, 'The Present Position of European Politics' (Chapman & Hall).

from securing all the advantages "of the marvellous fertility of the Heri Rud," as a base for acting against India.

We are to yield every sort of advantage to Russia for the attack on India, because "the highest authorities" have decided that we cannot attack Russia in Europe. We assert emphatically, that just as the "highest authorities" in relation to cavalry action mean, for Sir Charles Dilke, as we showed in our first article, "those who agree with me," and do not mean the men of European reputation, or the men whose arguments have been laid before the military opinion of Europe, and have been universally accepted as sound by those whose judgments decide it, so in relation to this far greater question, the " highest authorities " do not mean the men who have been tried and have proved their value, but do mean either those who have not been tried, those who have failed, or those who have had no opportunities for knowing the evidence on this question. It is naturally not the business of *Indian* authorities, however high, to obtain information as to the best points for attacking Russia in Europe.

It is because the power of attacking Russia in Europe is vital to us that the question of the "balance of military power in Europe" is a matter that concerns us so nearly.

So far as we have gone at present in discussing that question, our purpose has been to show—

1. That the reform of our military forces which is at present in progress, is of the kind which will enable us most economically to utilise the strength we possess and to defend our empire.

2. That we cannot keep India in economical and tranquil security, even if we can defend it at all, without the power of striking effective blows against Russia elsewhere than from India.

3. That we at present do not spend upon our forces sums incomparably greater than foreign Powers do, but that on the contrary our monetary sacrifices are much less than those of foreign Powers, although we have a far more vulnerable and a vastly more extended empire than any other Power whatever, and though we do not make any of those personal sacrifices which are involved in compulsory service.

4. That unless this be recognised, it is hopeless to attempt to provide an army relatively economical and efficient, because our actual deficiencies, as to which all men are agreed, are so very serious that only by increased expenditure can they be remedied.

5. That our present system of expenditure has not been an economical one, because it has been headless, unreasoned, inorganic, haphazard — designed to furnish War Ministers with effective

speeches for the House of Commons, and not designed by any men who could really and effectively combine power and responsibility; because power and knowledge have been hopelessly divorced, because every department has catered for itself, and no one for all.

6. That in the present condition of the Continent, the great central and conservative Power of Germany is undoubtedly still, by frontiers, by position, by organisation, by military training and force, the strongest in Europe. That to her Austria is a necessity; and that, though Austria is not as strong as Russia, her forces would have probably many elements of strength in such a contest which she has often lacked in former wars. That France is undoubtedly immeasurably stronger than she was in 1870, but that there are elements of uncertainty in her military organisation such as there are not in Germany. We may add now that those uncertainties have not been removed by her recent very limited and long-prepared mobilisation, and that the new military law has at least introduced a new element of uncertainty as to her strength. That Russia, from the enormous numbers of her population, and from the extent to which she devotes all her resources to preparation for war, must always be a great military Power; but that she has not gained, but lost very heavily indeed, by the changed conditions of modern war-

fare. That, till she has again had to fight with a European Power, it will be impossible absolutely to estimate her military strength; but that, though she has been actively engaged since 1877 in perfecting her military organisation, yet the weaknesses which she showed in the Turkish war were due not merely to temporary defects, but to conditions inherent in the nature of her people and her Government. That, nevertheless, her special aptitude for assimilating an Eastern people, and so rolling up her strength as she advances towards India, is a real power, and to us a real danger. That that advance is no result of accident, or of such causes as those which have, in the teeth of every sort of effort of the Home Government to restrain the tendency, led to the extension of our Indian empire. That the notion that that is so is simply the result of ignorant, cosmopolitan, easy-going pseudo-liberality of mind in England. That the advance has been designed from St Petersburg, and has been concealed by every artifice.

7. That under those circumstances our interest lies, not in insular exclusiveness, but in joining hands with those who have as much interest as we have in opposing the designs of Russia. That for us, therefore, the central point of the balance of power in Europe lies in the relations of other Powers to Russia.

8. In our last article we examined the counter-

weights, Germany and France. Incidentally we there showed why we do not believe that there is any reason for fear lest either of them will be greatly tempted to violate the neutrality of Belgium, provided Belgium performs her duty; that we shall earn no gratitude either from Germany or France by not fulfilling international obligations to Belgium to which we stand distinctly pledged; and that certainly no one has had authority to declare that we intend to break our word.

In our next and final article, we propose to examine certain questions as to our own possible alliances, and more especially to consider the effect upon the European balance of the rise of the young and vigorous Power of Italy, and the condition of Turkey, and to say a few words about China. We shall then be able to lead up to our general conclusion as to our future policy based upon the considerations we have urged.

IV.

ITALY, TURKEY, AND ENGLISH ALLIANCES

ITALY, TURKEY, AND ENGLISH ALLIANCES.

WE have now to deal with what seems to us to be for Englishmen the most important factor in the whole European problem. Writing, as we have been throughout, purely from a national and in no wise from a party point of view, it would be both ungracious and unfair not to acknowledge that, in our judgment, we very largely owe the national advantage to us of the rise of the Italian power to one man—Mr Gladstone. Probably no man ever more completely expressed the feeling of sympathy of one great nation for another than did Mr Gladstone, when he declared in 1860 that there was a subject on which all Englishmen everywhere were agreed—"that Italy ought to be one; that Italy ought to be free." It was many years after that before Italians as a nation fully realised the extent and depth of the sympathy which had been felt for them in England. They have very fully realised it now. Such matters are of the gravest possible importance. It seems to us that no word should be said in England which can in any way tend to modify that friendly feeling.[1]

Yet there is, apart altogether from historical sympathy, a service which England can now render to Italy such as it has never before been possible for England to render to any Power possessed of a great national army. England can at one and the same time secure Italy from attack, and can enable her to become an offensive Power. That is a consideration for statesman rather than for peoples, but it is essential for us that our people should understand it. What is perhaps of even more importance to us is, that this fact is thoroughly realised by Italian statesmen of all parties, and by the more influential and intelligent classes throughout the country. We almost fear lest, in the space of an article in which we have much else to discuss, we shall not be able to bring fully home to our English readers in detail the causes which make this a military and political certainty. Briefly stated, it is clear enough that a country with an enormous seaboard, a country of length without

[1] We regret that in Sir Charles Dilke's article in the November 1887 number of the 'Fortnightly,' he should have thought it necessary to discuss the possible injury which English hostility might inflict on Italy. Is it wise for a politician to discuss such a subject at all in regard to a friendly and most sensitive country?

breadth, dependent for a large portion of its forces on two islands, and divided throughout the length of its mainland by a great mountain-chain, is liable to invasion from France by sea to an extent to which she is not liable to invasion across a mountain-range the defence of which has been elaborately prepared. The consequence of these facts is, that the debates in the Italian Parliament, the pamphlets which have teemed from the Italian press, and the innumerable discussions which have testified to the intense patriotic interest which all Italians have taken in the question of national welfare, all turn upon this point. As we shall probably more easily convince our readers by a few extracts of the intensity of this feeling, than we shall drive home a proof of some military intricacy as to facts about a foreign country, we venture to give the following.

Here is the first, from 'Nuova Antologia' of October 1884: "With our present resources we can defend ourselves, but we cannot conquer. . . . We must be prepared to see, at the beginning of hostilities, our coasts and seas infested by war-ships, which will capture ships, destroy railways, and attempt surprises and attacks of all sorts. If we are not prepared to do the same, we shall be surprised, crushed, and exposed to incalculable disasters."

Here is a soldier's view. Lieut.-General Ricci, late Chief of the Staff of the Italian army, on returning from a tour of inspection at Massouah, said to his constitutents at Belluno: "Our continental frontier is one of the strongest in the world, because the Alps, fortified as they are, and defended by 250,000 or 300,000 Italians, present an impassable barrier. I even dare say that we are too strong on the side of the Alps, and I wish to again ask the Chamber to economise here as much as possible in order to increase the naval budget, so that we may have enough ships to prevent attack on our coasts, *the weak point—very weak point—of Italy.* . . . Each time that I, General of the Army, and Alpine deputy, appear in Parliament, I shall say, 'All for the navy.'"

These extracts, which might be multiplied indefinitely, are only representative of what is the universal Italian feeling. The difficulty is to convey to English readers the impression which is left upon those who have most closely been watching what has been going on in the peninsula of the "zeal and untiring energy with which Italy has pressed forward her land and sea defences: it is necessary to take stock of the multitudinous improvements in every service, and to study the frequent and instructive debates, to acquire a true idea of the immense interest taken in this question by all classes." We quote from a private letter from Captain A'Court, the author of 'Military Italy,' who has devoted years to the patient study of this question. His book is now by far the most complete account we have of the actual condition of the military forces of the kingdom.

For our purposes it will be sufficient to say that by the laws of 1882 the Italian army having been increased by 150,000 men, and the army-corps increased from ten to twelve, she has now 430,000 men actually available in the army, with 200,000 "mobile militia" in second line ready to reinforce them. Allowing for the complete defence of the Alpine region, according to a scheme elaborated by General Ricci, she has available 330,000 men for active operations in the field, either against Russia in support of Austria or against France in support of Germany,—*provided, and provided only, that an alliance with a great naval Power secures the Italian coasts.*

With all the efforts that Italy has made to strengthen her navy, she does not at all disguise from herself that the French navy is incomparably stronger. Nor is it only the French navy that she has to fear by sea. When we have spoken of two army-corps and a cavalry division as representing the force which at least we ought to have ready to ship, and have declared that at least until that force has been provided complete in all respects and ready to act, no other additions to our army would serve our turn, we take account of the immense distance to which it would be necessary for us to transport troops. The vast increase in the supplies of all kinds which are involved in long sea-transits multiplies, to an extent that would hardly be believed, the amount of mercantile tonnage that is required. The few hours' steaming which intervene between France and Italy impose altogether other conditions of sea-transport. Paper transport by sea for those who have not actually taken up the tenders, is apt to seem a much simpler thing than it does to those who have to provide, even for a few days, for all that troops require on landing. It will, however, at least give some indication of what Italians fear, if we say that Colonel Perrucretti, in 'La Difesa dello stato,' one of the most popular of Italian works, calculates that France has the means of forming and rapidly transporting by sea four army-corps. It is not too much to say that if that is true, or anything like true, the mere danger of such a descent on some unknown point of the Italian coast, together with the command of the sea by the French fleet, would be sufficient to paralyse the entire Italian army that could be spared from the local defence of the Alps. Thus a French force numerically most inferior to the Italian army would be sufficient to prevent Italy either from assisting Austria or troubling France.

To sum up—the Italians have, with one exception which we shall presently note,[1] no fear of not being able to hold their own perfectly as long as

[1] *Vide* p. 226.

the contest is confined to movement across the respective land-frontiers. Without an English alliance the entire Italian army would be paralysed for offensive action by the French fleet and a comparatively small portion of the French army. With an English alliance the combined Italian and Mediterranean fleets would certainly command the sea, paralyse any possible attempt at French invasion by sea, protect the much exposed Italian ports, many of which, like Naples, are not only unprotected, but from local causes cannot be adequately protected, and finally would set free the Italian army for action beyond the frontiers. We say, therefore, that the rise of the Italian Power has completely changed the relation of a great naval Power like England to the military forces of the Continent. Without putting a soldier on shore abroad, and without moving a soldier from England, we can by our naval action alone, and that without any special strain on our naval forces, set free at least 300,000 men for effective action against the aggressive Powers of the Continent.

It seems to us that under these circumstances the principle of all our policy ought to be, before all things, an active alliance with Italy. No one who has studied the views of Italian statesmen can fail to see that that is their opinion also. An alliance of Italy with Germany, or even of Italy with Germany and Austria, without an English alliance against Russia and France, is of the nature of the alliance of Thumblin with the giant, in which Thumblin gets all the knocks. Not that we do not think Italy a great Power. Italy and England allied together become two very great Powers indeed, from the moment that England has provided the force which is indispensable for the security of her own existence. But no alliance that Germany or Germany and Austria can offer to Italy, will save her from what Italians know to be their real danger. Germany and Austria, having to deal with the Russian navy, cannot absorb a sufficient portion of the activity of the French fleet to make Italy safe.

There is no alliance which would so securely unite all parties in this country. If it be true, as Sir Charles Dilke alleges in his article in the 'Fortnightly' of November 1887, that Prince Bismarck has recently proposed to England to join the three Powers, the cause is clear. Either Signor Crispi's interview or the views of Italian statesmen, expressed through other means, have made him attach a different value to the "sick old woman" from that which it suited his policy to profess in former times. It is clear that England and Italy together can offer to the central Powers an accession of strength which Bismarck could not and does not despise. It is equally clear that he cannot get Italy to join him on the same terms without our alliance. This fact changes the nature of our power in relation to every state on the Continent. We do not believe, as we have already shown, that Italy is, as Sir Charles Dilke alleged, so necessary to the existence of Austria that Austria must cringe to her to any extent to secure her alliance; but this much is certain, that Italy cannot move a man to the support of Austria without our alliance. The position of France in any contest between Russia and Austria is so menacing for Italy, that neutrality is enforced on Italy, at least until Germany and France are at war. Even then we think we have given reasons for believing that whilst the French fleet holds the seas, Italy will scarcely be able to move. Therefore to Austria our adhesion to the alliance is vital in proportion as the alliance of Italy is or is not important to her. As Sir Charles Dilke has at least given its full weight to the value of that alliance, the importance of which for Austria we by no means ignore, we claim his evidence as representing on that side the value we can offer to Austria on the *do ut des* principle. We have much else also to offer her, of which it will be more convenient to speak later.

Having this view of the importance and effect of Italian alliance before us, we wrote in our first article: "It is *almost* certain that we shall never have to enter into any quarrel in which *we cannot obtain* allies, to whom the command of the sea, such a force[1] so capable of movement, and the financial support of England, would be of priceless value."[2] We do not think that these words, used after we had referred to the importance of Italy, and had repeatedly spoken of acting on the *do ut des* principle, conveyed to any one else the impression which they did to Sir Charles Dilke. "He is *positive*, however," he says of the present writer— "and I envy him his firm belief—that *when war comes upon us* we shall have allies." If they had done so, they would have been ill-chosen words. A forced construction placed on an isolated clause in a long argument is apt to mislead; but as it is vital to us not to be misunderstood in this matter, we are much more anxious to make our meaning clear than to split hairs as to the correct turn of a phrase. The purpose, then, with which we undertook these articles may now be fully stated, and the argument as a whole worked out. We do not believe, and never have believed, that if we wait till war comes upon us in behalf of our own interests, we can secure allies who will fight for us when we have refused to fight for them. We believe, as Sir Charles Dilke believes, that a great

---

[1] Two army-corps and a cavalry division complete in all respects, and ready to embark on the word being given.

[2] *Vide* p. 51. I retain here the wording of the original article as it has been challenged by Sir C. Dilke. I have for the sake of greater clearness slightly altered it at p. 51.

change has come over the political relation of England to the Continent since we have in Asia come to have frontiers which virtually march with those of a great European Power. We believe that the phase of public opinion which looked upon it as the duty of English statesmen to keep clear of Continental alliances, and to devote our strength to the peaceful extension of our colonial empire, was a very natural and legitimate view of the existing condition of things for many years of the present century. We believe also with Sir Charles Dilke that in our days it is impossible for English statesmen, however clearly they may see that the circumstances which tended to form a certain popular sentiment have radically changed, to commit the country to action for which it is not prepared. We do not see how, as an upright statesman who desired to pledge himself to brother statesmen on the Continent to that only which he could fulfil to the letter, it would have been possible for Lord Salisbury to completely commit this country to a formal union with the great peace-league of the three Powers. Therefore we firmly believe that, in order that such alliance, which is now vital to our interests, should be formed, the nation generally must have laid before them the motives which ought to determine our action. It is well that our foreign policy should be consistent, continuous, and based on a knowledge of the existing state of things, which prevents violent changes when one party succeeds another in power. Circumstances, however, alter cases. The policy which was wise, or appeared wise, to the majority of Englishmen under one condition of things, may, if they see clearly that those conditions have altogether changed, appear in a very different light to them. There is no reason why English opinion should not be roused to the same interest in the question which exists at this moment everywhere throughout Italy. Therefore we held it to be our duty, having facts before us which, as we have heard from all sides, have not hitherto been understood by most Englishmen, to lay them before them.

We think we do Sir Charles Dilke no injustice when we say that the whole purport of his articles was to leave the impression that war with Russia being sooner or later inevitable for us, and war with Russia and France together a by no means impossible contingency, we must prepare ourselves to fight them without allies. He based that opinion on the belief that our alliance was not worth having, and that the rejection of it by Austria at Prince Bismarck's instigation, which he alleged had at the beginning of the year recently occurred, was representative of what we had to expect for the future.[1] We said, therefore, when we first challenged his

---

[1] Compare 'The Present Position of European Politics,' pp. 16, 21, 160, 185, 186 *et seq.*, with p. 277 and pp. 339-343.

statements, and we say now, that both in the case of England and Russia he put strength for weakness and weakness for strength. We entirely agree with those military critics who have assured him that he has underrated the power of Russia, and exaggerated the power of England, in maintaining that by some tinkering with our military finances, by some catching at popular military prejudices, by some substituting of a plausible statesman who is "out" for one who is in, we can more easily arrange to meet Russia in the field, in India, or at Vladivostock, without allies, than we can arrange to meet her elsewhere with them.[1] We say that he exaggerated the power of Russia when he tried to persuade us to leave the nations of the Continent to be trodden under the feet of the colossus because Russia, or, at all events, Russia and France together, represented a force so great that other nations could not resist them. We say that he misjudged the statesmanship of Italian statesmen when he believed that their whole policy was one of *pourboires*.

We believed then, and believe now, that the position in which we stand is very much like that in which Prussia stood in the years prior to 1806, whilst Napoleon was overthrowing Austria and the other states of the Continent. We can fan our-

[1] Sir C. Dilke has challenged the fairness of this statement. My answer lies in the references given on the preceding page.

selves with the belief that it is a matter of no moment to us whether Russia and France do or do not deal first with the Continental Powers, and then with ourselves. In that case we shall surely be left, as Prussia was in 1806, without allies when the fast-approaching hour arrives when Russia is able to deal with us in India, secure at least in a neutrality of France benevolent towards her, and ready to take every advantage of her many causes of quarrel with us. On the other hand, if only our fleet be in the condition in which all Englishmen desire to see it, we can offer such additional strength to the alliance of Germany, Austria, and Italy, that we ought to be able to make such terms as will keep Russia and France quiet and at peace both with ourselves and the other Powers for our generation and perhaps the next. We neither deny nor affirm that our fleet is now in that condition. That is a question for sailors. It happens now, as it often happens, that the questions of the nature of the great services which a fleet can render us are mainly dependent on points of military study on land. It is because of the nature of the military frontiers of Germany and Russia, and of the military forces and lines of communication of the two great empires, that we are able to affirm that, by prohibiting a Russian naval expedition against Königsberg, Memel, and Danzig, the Whale can offer a direct service to the Prussian Eagle against the Elephant that may be worth the Eagle's purchasing at a price.[1] It is because of the necessary military distribution of the Italian depots, fortresses, and frontiers that we are able to affirm that our navy can offer a service to Italy which will affect Germany and Austria alike, and be worth at least 300,000 men to the alliance. Whether our navy can at this moment crush or confine the now nearly ready Russian fleet in the Black Sea, and at the same time, with the assistance of the Italian fleet, dominate the Mediterranean and the Baltic, while it secures our commerce, our shores, and our colonies from attack, we do not know. From a military point of view, those are the services it ought to render us. Till it can accomplish them with certainty, we cry with General Ricci, "All for the navy and nothing for the army." To that, however, there is one saving clause on which we need not dwell, as on that point we are in entire agreement with Sir Charles Dilke. The army knows perfectly what the navy requires from it in order to accomplish its proper work at sea—secure ports, and secure coaling-stations. Their security is imperative if we are to be able to feed our population in time of war.

We shall, however, continue to accuse Sir Charles Dilke, in season and out of season, of party spirit, until he acknowledges one fact on

[1] See III., "Germany, Russia, and Austria."

that matter, which is true whether he acknowledges it or not. The one statesman who has really and heartily thrown himself into the cause of practically securing for us coaling-stations and harbours effectively garrisoned, and has gone as far in it as it was possible for a man to do, has not been Sir Charles Dilke, has not been Mr Stanhope, or any other statesman, Conservative or Liberal, but Mr Smith. Sir Charles Dilke either knows that or is wilfully ignorant of it. For our part, in so far as any feeling of the kind affected our determination to offer these articles to our readers, it was the sense of the mischief to the country that was done when a statesman not much given to talk, but steadily and honestly setting himself to work at reforms not showy but vital to efficieny, was assailed by a clever talker, appealing to every catch-penny prejudice that could be raked together. Those reforms have been now fully explained in public by General Brackenbury; and we are at a loss to understand how Sir Charles Dilke can say, after expressing the fullest approval of them, that he does not know what was meant when, speaking of this work, which had then at Mr Smith's instance, and with his full approval, been just accomplished, Lord Wolseley declared that more effective, non-theatrical work had been done in them than he had known done for years. Sir

Charles Dilke wishes those who desire genuine army reform not to hit at one another. We heartily sympathise with the wish; but the speech from him seems to us like the historical one of the robber to the policeman, to which we can only give the policeman's answer. The present writer never once spoke to Mr Smith. Not a word of what has been here written in Mr Smith's praise would have been altered had he been a Radical statesman, if that statesman had shown the desire Mr Smith has shown to accomplish genuine work for the country. We have had enough and to spare of brilliant speeches made by Secretaries of State for War, for which they receive the compliments of every one in the House. A little steady, unstagey, untheatrical work, that does not show in a speech, is a novelty; and, whilst Sir Charles Dilke shows his patriotism and independence of party spirit by vituperating or undervaluing all work, no matter how valuable it has been, done whilst Conservatives happened to be in power, we shall show ours by throwing all the enthusiasm we can into the support of any statesman, no matter of what party, who will strive after genuine efficiency.

Since we began our series there has appeared an article[1] from the pen of Herr von Bunsen, declaring, not as an expression of his own opinion

---

[1] 'Nineteenth Century,' Sept. 1887—"A German View of Mr Gladstone."

but as a study of the growth of public opinion in Germany, that the Germans generally have come to look upon this question as we do. He says that the whole feeling of Germany towards England has undergone a change, precisely because they consider that the great danger of the present situation lies in the high probability that, whether from deliberate design or as a consequence of the course of events, Russia and France together may attack England by herself first without allies, or else may attack Germany and Austria by themselves. We have in the present article shown why it is the case that these great military Powers may well desire the alliance of England, even though she should not be able to land a single *corps d'armée* anywhere. Herr von Bunsen belongs to a family of statesmen, and is not likely to write without knowing what the views of German statesmen are. This article, the speeches which have been made in the Foreign Committee of the Hungarian Delegations, notably on November 5, together with Signor Crispi's declarations, have been sufficient to refute Sir Charles Dilke's statement that "we are so little prepared for war *that no Power thinks our alliance worth having* for a short war, and it is the first days of a war that count at the present time."[1] But if these be not sufficient, Sir Charles's present assertion that Prince Bismarck has recently

---

[1] The Present Position of European Politics, p. 160.

pressed upon us an alliance with the three Powers, is its complete and final refutation.[1]

We entirely agree with Sir Charles that the first days of a war are now of vital importance. We entirely agree with him that our army is not now ready for the first few days or weeks, hardly for the first few months, of a Continental war. It has been with a view to make it so, that all the reforms which Sir Charles Dilke has so fiercely attacked were being attempted.[2] If he can use his influence with Radical members to give courage to the Government to ask for the immediate expenditure which he now at last admits to be necessary in order to carry them out, he will confer the greatest service on his country which lies in his power.

Nevertheless with our army as it is, though we cannot do all that we ought to be able to do for the defence of the country, we can act potently on the first few days of a Continental war, as we cannot act on the first few days of a war between ourselves and Russia. A telegraphic order to our Mediterranean fleet to join the Italian navy will then and there set free at least 300,000 soldiers in Italy from the moment they are mobilised, and

[1] Fortnightly Review, November 1887.
[2] I do not myself profess to reconcile the apparent approval of General Brackenbury's speech, alluded to on p. 206, and the attack on the very same reforms which was the basis of Sir Charles Dilke's article on "The United Kingdom."

will begin to operate with enormous force in favour of the great alliance during the course of the very days of mobilisation. A telegraphic assurance to Germany that another English fleet will co-operate with the German from the moment that the state of the Baltic permits the Russian fleet to approach Memel, Königsberg, or Danzig, will enable the German leaders completely to modify all their plans for dealing with Russia. It will secure the communications of a German army engaged in the invasion of Poland. It will protect Germany on the only side on which Russian attack could be seriously dangerous.[1] Before we conclude our article, we shall show that yet another telegraphic order will be worth a further 200,000 men to Germany. There is no Power in Europe whose influence can be so rapidly exercised.

Therefore, *pace* Sir Charles Dilke, we say that, with these weapons in our hands, it will be not in war-power but in statesmenship and diplomacy that England will fail, if we are not able to make such terms with other States as will oblige Russia to leave Herat alone. We feel certain that if only our statesmen will take to heart that principle which Sir Charles Dilke has so soundly and wisely pressed on them, that at present they must understand the conditions of war on the Continent if

---

[1] For the complete justification for these statements, see III., "Germany, Russia, and Austria."

they would attempt to safeguard England, there are yet other terms that we can make. We believe that Russia could be held to adhere, in relation to all the points of interest to us as well as to Europe, to the bargains she has made. We believe that we could obtain security that her pledges so habitually broken, and her solemn words so habitually repudiated, shall not again be ignored. Only by the union of the four Powers, all interested in peace, can such a result be secured.

We believe, also, that we could obtain a very similar security as against France. We wish that Sir Charles Dilke had brought out more fully than he has done many of those causes of quarrel with France to which he has only alluded. We fear that our diplomacy will only be too willing to continue the evil courses in which it has been for more than a generation engaged, trusting to the ignorance of the nation as to the feeble concessions about which Sir Charles has only given hints.

We wish that he had drawn attention to the almost appalling frankness with which law officers of the Crown have declared that on the coast of Newfoundland, thanks to the carelessness and neglect of our statesmen, we have allowed French "rights of user" to be converted into "rights of wont," and "rights of wont" to be converted into tolerated claims to exclusive possession, till now, in a territory where the French have not, by treaty, a yard of soil, the French newspapers talk of "the French coast," almost as if they had territorial jurisdiction over it and we had not. How long it will be before French diplomatists adopt the same tone it would be dangerous to predict. An alliance for the maintenance of treaty rights, by which the rights of all the four Powers concerned were mutually guaranteed, and the violations of treaty were regarded as a matter of common interest, would give a firmness to our diplomacy and a security to peace such as there has not been in the world, at least since what Sir Charles Dilke now says that he agrees with us in thinking our great blunder in 1864, though he considers us most partisan writers for having called it so.

For it must not be disguised that the situation, as it now stands, though it is most satisfactory for the central Powers, is most dangerous for us. It is true that the Hungarian representatives have shown that they appreciate the nature of the action of English statesmen in a way that, unfortunately, it would be thought derogatory to the dignity of an English Opposition on either side to admit that they appreciated it. "We expect," said Csernatony, "no formal alliance on the part of England, as it is her habit not to bind herself before she finds it necessary to go to war; but it is highly satisfactory to learn that England is not against us, and will never side with our enemies; and that her goodwill towards us, from which we may derive great advantages, is assured."

Unfortunately the "semi-alliance" which may confer these great advantages on the central Powers offers us no guarantee of their help in an event which that semi-alliance itself is especially likely to bring about.

Sir Charles Dilke thinks that nihilism would disappear if Russia went to war. We gladly accept his authority on a subject of which he knows much more than we do. It is at least certain that the probability that war would kill nihilism is sufficiently strong to make war present continual temptations to the Tzar. Is it not likely, then, that the very strength of the alliance of the three Powers, with England in the background, may induce the Tzar now to turn his attention towards India, instead of towards Europe? Unless we have made not a "half alliance" but a whole alliance with the other Powers, so that they are as much pledged to us as we to them, he will there find England in the foreground with no other Powers behind her. Nor, unless the declarations which Lord Hartington used formerly to make are wholly unsound, would the result be very different if the Tzar were to turn his attention to Asia Minor instead of to India. "In Asia Minor," as Lord Hartington used to say, "lies the great danger for England." In either case, as Sir Charles Dilke himself admits, it would be at least highly probable that we should have France on our back at the same time. Why should we run this tremendous risk merely for the sake of preserving a pedantic tradition of English statesmanship, suited to conditions which are not those of to-day? Why should we be compelled to put our armed forces on an enormously expensive establishment? For the discovery that Sir Charles Dilke has now made, that we must at least begin with an expenditure of several millions, shows only that he now knows of a flea-bite on what it will actually cost us to be ready, out of our own resources alone, to face Russia and France together, as he admits that with the policy which he advocates we must be ready to do.

Towards the end of the Franco-German war, when M. Thiers—the old war-historian of France, the great exponent of the Napoleonic tradition as to war, the author of the fortifications of Paris—was endeavouring to persuade his countrymen for the moment to make peace, he used an argument which seems to us worth considering in our present situation. "If," he said, "four men better armed than I am come to me and demand my purse, I do not choose the moment when they are superior to me to settle the question finally. I make such terms with them as I can for the moment, and then I go to six other men as much interested as I am in stopping robbery, and arrange with them to master the robbers and recover my purse." We are in a somewhat happier position. Two are threatening a general disturbance. If they can only catch one alone, they are quite ready to tackle him for their common advantage. Three of those exposed to this risk are agreed in lending one another mutual support. We, the fourth, stand apart, wishing well to the three, and very likely to be obliged to join them if the three are attacked. The three are most anxious that we should join them, and are quite ready to give as we give. But we have, and can have, no counter-promise from them, because, though our feelings are sufficiently well known to the other two to irritate them greatly, we prefer sitting half on one side and half on the other of the fence, and will not make up our mind to a definite decision. Is that for us a satisfactory condition of things? Can it foreshadow any good for us?

Nor is even that a full statement of the case. As we have shown in our detailed examination of the facts, we can, for the purposes of the general alliance, use our own special strength to the full. If we allow ourselves to be isolated and then attacked, instead of being able to lend offensive power to the general service, we shall be thrown upon a miserable defensive. With Russia we shall find, as we did in the days of the Crimea, that we cannot exert our naval power to its full extent, and must trust to the service in which we shall be always weakest. When Sir Charles Dilke has done his utmost to expand our forces to the dimensions of the great Continental armies,[1] we fear much that the faithful son must say to his country what the little frog of Æsop's fable said to his mother, attempting to blow herself out to the size of the ox—"You will burst before you succeed." We can be, relatively to other countries, as great a naval Power as we choose to be. We shall be delighted if from Sir Charles, or any one else, we can hear of any means that will economically increase the size of our army. We are bound, however, to say that, if what he has in his articles foreshadowed be the solution he is about to propose to us, then there is much danger lest he should increase numbers without increasing force. He speaks of an English system not based upon foreign schemes. We are delighted with all genuine thought and genuine originality. We fear, however, that he has already given us hints enough to show that the scheme he is to propose is one that has been already tried and discarded because of its failure by a great Continental Power. However, we shall be anxious to hear without prejudice what his proposals are. In

[1] I, in common with others, have so understood him. But, as the burial service puts it, "he continueth not in any one stay," so that it is difficult to be sure what his actual meaning is. He now says that this does not represent his view.

the meantime, we do not think it will be easy to persuade Englishmen that a contest in which their naval power cannot be freely exerted can ever be so satisfactory a one for them as one in which naval power tells from the first outbreak of war.

There is, however, one argument which has been recently very ably put in the 'Spectator' against the possibility of our forming an alliance such as we have described. The writer urges that we cannot adhere as patiently and consistently to a formed purpose as is the case with Powers ruled by a despot. Is that historically true? We do not think so. Of all the Powers opposed to Napoleon, which maintained the struggle with most patience and consistency?

Nor can we persuade ourselves that the more aristocratic nature of our constitution in those days materially affected the question. The feelings of all classes were as heartily enlisted in that struggle as were those of the ruling men—nay, it was the popular feeling which originally forced Pitt's unwilling hand. But if that be not a sufficient indication of the extent to which a country with a very popular constitution may adhere firmly to a policy once thoroughly understood by the mass of the nation, what case can be more forcible than that of the United States of America during the war with the South? What comparisons are naturally suggested by the setting of that case side by side with the action of the Russian armies in the days of Frederick the Great! Then the successive deaths of Russian rulers converted on the spot enemies into friends, friends into enemies. What reversals of policy that, at the worst, England has ever known, approach in their suddenness the changes which are suggested by the mere names, Elizabeth, Paul, Catherine? It appears to us that the whole history of the English race, both in America and England, promises, despite some lapses due to the violence of party spirit,[1] a security to allies not to be found elsewhere. It is of equal importance to us that the belief that that is so is strong on the Continent. Even now, in the Foreign Committee of the Hungarian Delegations, the independent members contrast the "sympathetic attitude of England" with "the frequently vacillating conduct of Germany." Few things can be more significant than Count Apponyi's speech on that matter on November 5th.

We turn, however, now to a question on which, as it seems to us, the Italian alliance offers us a solution of a difficulty which more than any other threatens to make it hard for us in England to maintain a continuous and persistent policy in

[1] We are disposed to agree with Mr Green that the worst case of which we have been ever guilty, the desertion of Frederick, was due chiefly to the personal wilfulness of the young king, George III., on his accession. Chatham surely then represented the popular feeling in favour of persistency.

foreign affairs. We hardly think that any one in England now doubts that pacha government in Asia Minor is intolerably bad. We hardly think that any one is ready to commit England to the defence of intolerably bad government. On the other hand, no Conservative statesman has ever been more strongly opposed to allowing Russian government to be substituted for Turkish, than were Mazzini and the most Liberal or Radical of Italian statesmen. Carl Blind's article, to which we have referred already,[1] supplies, to those who are not cognisant of these facts, unanswerable evidence on that subject. Notoriously Signor Crispi is the heir of these traditions, and not of any mere historical or selfish policy for the maintenance of the integrity of the Turkish empire. Bad as pacha government may be, it is at least subject to a pressure from without which tends to check its worst excesses. We would ask any one who thinks that there may not be something worse than this to study Prince Kropotkine's new work.[2] We cannot believe that Englishmen, who appreciate the check to tyranny which is supplied by ample daylight, can doubt that a Government which can work out in absolute darkness such devilry as Prince Kropotkine proves to be common, would

---

[1] P. 137, *ante*.
[2] In Russian and French Prisons. By Prince Kropotkine. London: Ward & Downey. 1887.

be a blessing even to Asia Minor. No statesmen are more heartily friendly than the Italian to the emancipated Balkan States. No one now doubts that friendliness towards them is the true policy of English statesmen, and that in the persons of Lord Salisbury and Lord Rosebery both parties are committed to that view. The policy of Russia towards Turkey is simple enough. It consists in pandering to the vices of the ruling pachas in order to make the government of Turkey as bad as possible, so that it may disgust Europe and become intolerable to the subjects of Turkey.[1] It seems to us that all English parties may agree in resisting to the utmost that policy. Surely also we may join Signor Crispi in refusing to allow Russia to be the heir of Turkey.

[1] Ignatieff, no doubt, in 1877 carried out that policy with a perfection that it never attained before or since. To have induced the repudiation of the debt, and by a subtle complication of ingenious intrigue to have almost compelled the Turkish Government to employ in the suppression of the insurrection he had fomented the local militia instead of the Turkish regulars, were masterpieces of their kind. The knowledge he thus showed of the possible devilries which the sectarian zeal of Bulgarian Verts might be trusted to work on men of their own race, with whom they had carried on a feud for centuries, was marvellous. His cynical appreciation of the effect of his action upon the conscience of Europe was only equalled by the cynicism with which he subsequently worked for political purposes the devilries of the Jew-baiting. In his person Russia decorated the supreme leader in both crimes. We have never been able to understand why the volume known as 'Les Responsabilités,' in which the whole story of Ignatieff's action at Constantinople was set forth, was never published or in any way made known in England.

We have dealt first with what we believe to be by far the more difficult problem involved in this question—the problem, that is, of adopting such a policy towards Turkey as may enable us to utilise her brave soldiers in the common resistance to Russian aggression, with the consent of Englishmen, who loathe as much as we do the wretched rule of the pachas in the outlying provinces of the Turkish empire. We do not in the least believe that it is necessary to commit ourselves to vague promises as to maintaining against her subject races the integrity of the empire in order to gain her assistance in keeping the Russians out of Asia Minor, or in inflicting such blows upon Russia, if she recommences the repudiation of treaties and the aggressive policy of the past, as will keep her quiet for many a long day. It is notorious that Turkey is now anxiously seeking admission into the Central Alliance. It will almost certainly not be granted to her—and we do not think that it ought to be granted to her on the terms on which other Powers enter into that alliance. Nevertheless it may be possible to agree with Turkey to assist her in preventing Russia from carrying out further aggression in Asia Minor, on condition of her assisting us in attacking the Russian lines of communication should Russia move on India.

On the side of Europe, Russia can now only approach Constantinople over the free Balkan

States, or by sea. We think Sir Charles Dilke will admit that towards a European prohibition of Constantinople to Russia on that side, we can lend, if not the most powerful assistance that any State can contribute, at least an aid which is second to none. That the English, Italian, and Turkish navies can, even when the very formidable fleet which Russia is providing in the Black Sea is complete, prohibit approach to Varna or Constantinople, ought not to be open to question. Whether that is an assistance which Roumania can offer in such an event to Austria, we shall not insult our readers by discussing.

We are not impressed by the knowledge as to the military facts of the 1877-78 campaign which has been shown by Sir Charles Dilke, whoever may have been his military advisers. He, in the form of a question, wishes to destroy the basis of an argument of ours, of some importance to the general position we have taken up. For the purpose of disclosing the weakness of his thesis, it will be convenient to extract from the question the logical position it involves.

Major premiss, — Some generals, who knew nothing of the condition of the Austrian and Prussian armies in 1866, felt sure that Austria must beat Prussia.

Minor premiss,—Yet Prussia beat Austria.

Therefore it is clear that no knowledge, however

complete, and however fully confirmed at present by historical documents, of the condition of the Russian army in Turkey in 1878, and of the strength of the English forces that could have been landed in the neighbourhood of Constantinople, can now enable any soldiers to say that in 1878 England was in a position to have prohibited Russian approach to Constantinople. Deduction, —Such fools are all soldiers! We shall not reply, but leave Lord Macaulay's schoolboy to do so.

The question, however, next arises, whether Italy and England can lend to Turkey a support in the Black Sea, and in Asia Minor, which will enable us to forbid Russian approach on the Asiatic side towards Constantinople, and to utilise the Turkish troops.

We should attach more importance to Sir Charles Dilke's very confident assertions of our impotence, if he had shown that he knew even a little of the present condition of the Turkish army. To judge of the prospects of a race or a battle from a knowledge of the efforts at training of only one of the competitors, is, after all, not to bet on a certainty. Sir Charles, from similar one-sided knowledge, evidently thinks that he is in that happy position. Now we have strong reason to believe that Turkey can even now put something like 300,000 effective soldiers, complete in all arms, into the field in Europe alone, without calling upon her Asiatic subjects. If that is so, considering that the far greater proportion of her fighting population resides in Asia Minor, it is not hard to believe, as we also have reason to think, that she is steadily working up to a standard, which will enable her to put an effective army, in all, more than 700,000 strong in the field.

We entirely agree with Sir Charles Dilke that if the numbers of the Turkish soldiery that can be provided out of this force to contend with Russia in Asia Minor are not adequate, we can add to them nothing in point of numbers that will justify us in speaking of protecting the Asiatic dominions of Turkey. But on the other hand, both Russia and Turkey know well that we more easily than any other Power can lend such aid in such a contest as will simply turn the scale of victory and defeat. We can enable Turkey to maintain her armies in the field in a country where efficiency of condition and facility of supply are more important than numbers, and where numbers that cannot be supplied and fed are utterly useless. We can supply officers that can be trusted, many of whom can speak Turkish. The two corps and the cavalry division of which we have spoken, serving as the nucleus of a force of Turks as large as the complete command of the sea would enable us to furnish and supply, would, in despite of Sir Charles Dilke's confident assertions, be able to act in those regions with decisive effect upon Russian action in India.

We know what we are talking about.[1] For the reasons we have already given, we utterly refuse to enter into further details for the benefit of our enemies. Here, as in the case of the European alliance, we say it is far better for us to develop and use such strength and force as may undoubtedly be ours, than to strain at the development of a force which will be delusive, and will involve us in confusion worse confounded. There is one principle which we venture to think we may at least learn from the Germans, if the commonsense of our own people does not furnish us with sufficient arguments for it—and that is, not to be perpetually reversing the methods on which we work with our army. One, if not the greatest misfortune which has hitherto attended the effort to bring our army up to the conditions of modern warfare, has been the necessity for providing successive Secretaries of State with the material for oratorical effects. The principles needed for the mobilisation of an army are now as well under-

---

[1] I retain this phrase, because I do not think it will be misunderstood by any one but Sir Charles Dilke. I mean simply that I deliberately abstain from entering into details because I do not think it would be right to enter into them, and not because I have not carefully considered the question, or have not had the means of knowing what those think who have had even better means of judging of it.

stood as the laws of the game of chess. What we want is to have them applied with business-like precision to our actual condition, as Mr Smith was striving to do during his unfortunately short tenure of the War Office. When we know what we want, the thing is actually to get it. We have endeavoured to show in what direction our efforts can be most economically and effectively employed. We feel a little disposed to borrow from a speech delivered some years ago by Mr Grant Duff, when member for the Elgin burghs. What we want from those who mean to have the army put on a sound basis is that they should "vote straight," and work to get others to "vote straight," not for a party but for the nation.

Before, however, we draw together the points which we are most anxious to enforce, we must recur to a matter to which we alluded when speaking of the defence of Italy on the land-frontier. There is a service to the cause of Italian defence which it ought not to be beyond the power of united European diplomacy to render her. Among the few remnants of the Treaty of Vienna, we think that most Englishmen assume that the neutrality of Switzerland has at least remained a part of the public law of Europe. Now, by one of the protocols of the Vienna Congress, "toutes les fois que les puissances voisines de la Suisse seront en hostilité ouverte ou imminente," Switzerland was authorised, for the purpose of neutralisation, to occupy the districts of Chablais, Faucigny, and other named parts of Savoy. Nothing in the transfer of Savoy and Nice to France in 1860 altered this condition of European law. Switzerland has recently claimed the right to execute this protocol in the event of imminent war. It is scarcely possible to exaggerate the importance to Italy of having this question at least settled on a clear basis. Upper Savoy in the possession of France, and with the free right to use it, allows a French army to menace Italian concentration in Piedmont by the Simplon, and to turn the Swiss defences by taking them in rear by Friburg and Berne, so as to fall upon the left flank of a German army between Basle and Schaffhausen. Clearly, both Italy and Germany have a right to understand whether this neutralised ground remains sacred from war or not. Left in the condition in which the question at present stands, with French troops trained to use this very ground in the teeth of treaties,[1] this nominal

---

[1] I do not, of course, mean that it is expressly contrary to treaty for French troops to be drilled on this ground, but that their local training to an employment of ground which would be valueless except by a violation of treaty is too significant not to suggest the purpose for which it is designed. It is a training to a use of this ground, which, if ever put into warlike practice, would be contrary to treaty. Sir Charles Dilke, in withdrawing a charge he had made of incorrectness against my statement, has declared that he looks upon the training of French troops in the military use of neutralised

neutralisation itself prevents either State from taking effective measures to protect themselves against the risk. It appears to us that we at least ought not to object to have any refusal to allow Switzerland to occupy this ground under the conditions of the protocol, considered as one of the *casus belli* which would be regarded as of common interest by all the members of the great alliance whose effective creation on fixed terms we desire.

As to China, we have little to add to what Sir Charles Dilke has said, except to express our strong agreement with him as to the importance to us of securing, as against Russia, that alliance in its most effective form. Nevertheless, we venture to think that here, as elsewhere, we must give if we wish to take. If it had been possible, with the full consent of China, to retain Port Hamilton —still more if it had been possible, with due regard to the vast number of our dispersed fortresses

ground as equivalent to "the training of Prussian guards at Potsdam." The difference between two kinds of military training is clearly a question for soldiers. I directly deny the soundness of Sir Charles Dilke's position, and I unhesitatingly submit the question to the military opinion of Europe. Drilling upon a parade-ground is one thing; local practice in the military knowledge of mountain-passes and a mountain district is another—one which can be only acquired in that district itself. The very acquisition of that special knowledge by troops becomes suspicious when it would be useless unless treaties were violated, and when a violation of treaty would give immense military advantage to the troops so trained. That is now the case in neutralised Savoy.

in distant seas and to their efficient defence, to make Port Hamilton into a strong fortress—we should have quite agreed with him as to the importance of gaining that foothold for enabling our fleet to cross any Russian movement from Vladivostock upon Australia. But we cannot believe that what Mr Carlyle used to call "præternatural suspicion" is the wise attitude for those who are not engaged in carrying on difficult negotiations as against those who are, so long as the critics are flying the banner of patriotism against party, and are appealing to their countrymen on those terms. Præternatural suspicion is, of course, the established function of "her Majesty's Opposition." So long as Sir Charles Dilke professes to write on party principles, these and many other strokes are intelligible enough. They are part of a game that we know. A Government has plenty of provision against such. What we object to is the sheep's-clothing of appeal to those who, like ourselves, do not accept those principles in a matter of national concern. Our own belief is, that whichever party had been in, Port Hamilton would have been surrendered when it was found that our occupation offended the Chinese.

Sir Charles Dilke thinks that, in maintaining that it is to the interest of England not to abandon Belgium if Belgium does not abandon herself, we have added further proof of the necessity for

revolutionary change in our military system.[1] We
believe, on the contrary, that the broad principle
which underlies our contention—the great alliance
for the maintenance of treaty rights—is the only
one which will enable us to maintain our empire
without changes which would affect to a revolutionary extent our domestic as much as our military
condition. England, known as the support of the
minor seaboard States, possesses a power which
she loses from the moment that she abandons that
position. We have said our say as to Belgium,
and shall not return to the subject; but there is
another question closely allied to it. If Denmark
has to choose between an alliance with France or
with Germany, the temptation to her to join France,
if only she thinks France strong enough to win,
must necessarily be very great. If Denmark has
to choose between an alliance with England and
Germany on one side and France on the other, it
is tolerably certain that she will be wise enough to
prefer the Anglo-German alliance. Nor does it, in
that case, seriously matter to any nation except
herself what decision she may arrive at in the
matter. Her neutrality, at least, would be enforced.
Now, as may be seen by any one who will refer to
the official history of the war of 1870, during the
earlier part of the war—that is, up to the end of
July—Germany, fully expecting that France would

[1] 'Fortnightly,' November 1887, p. 610.

attempt an incursion by sea, retained the whole mobilised force of the 1st, 2d, 4th, and 5th Corps —that is, at least 120,000 men—ready to meet such an invasion. Denmark is able to put about 60,000 men behind very effective fortifications in a country hard to invade. Now, suppose France and Russia—having full command of the sea— ship, as they well may, to a friendly country 50,000 men each to reinforce the Danish 60,000, we have an army of 160,000 men, with indefinite possibilities of reinforcement, concentrated in a position whence they could strike straight for Berlin and the heart of the German Empire.

It must be remembered that in all that we have said as to our disbelief as to the overwhelming forces which Russia could employ against Germany or Austria, the single reason we have alleged has been the difficulty of movement and supply. There is no question as to the vast number of troops which Russia has available. Therefore we think we shall be understood when we say that the troops which Russia could thus ship to Denmark, however numerous they ultimately became, would subtract nothing from the numbers she could pour directly over the German frontier. Yet for Germany the whole of this danger vanishes when she has secured the English alliance. We are convinced that we understate the fact when we say that, in any war against Russia and France,

Germany must, for the defence of her coasts and to fend herself from the risks of such an attack as we have described, subtract 200,000 men from her armies of the East and West. Therefore here is a figure of at least 200,000 men whom we can add to the militant forces available for the central alliance. Moreover, here as elsewhere we can act quicker than any other Power. From the moment that our alliance is known to be secured, all danger of this Russo-Franco-Danish action based on Denmark vanishes. German generals can work out their campaign at once with the full addition of the 200,000 men whom otherwise they must subtract from offensive war.

We have now stated our case. We have shown—

1. That, by the assistance we can afford to Italy, by protecting the German coasts, and by forbidding Denmark to lend herself as a base to Russia and France, we can give to the central alliance a support which is worth more to it than half a million of men. *More* than that number, because the question of Memel, Königsberg, and Danzig is not included in that estimate.

2. That we can also contribute more than our share towards protecting Constantinople and Varna from attack on the European side, because the easiest approach to both of them is by sea. We have left it to our readers to judge for themselves

whether the complete possession of the Black Sea, as against the complete loss of it, would not be worth to Austria something of importance in addition to this assistance.

3. Whether, when we have these advantages to offer her, Germany is likely to care to violate Belgian territory if we object to her doing so, we leave it to our readers to determine. As a question of the principle of maintaining treaty rights, which is the single principle on which a secure alliance can be based, we think that if Belgium fulfils her part, we ought not to abandon her, and that our abandonment of her would greatly weaken us.

4. In all that we have spoken of above, we have almost exclusively insisted upon what our navy can do if it is as strong as it ought to be. If, in addition to the above, we can place a small but highly organised force of two *corps d'armée* and a cavalry division where we please, on the outbreak of war, and can supply what is needed to render the Turkish forces effective to resist Russia, we believe we shall be in a condition to make such terms with other Powers as will prevent either Russia or France from attacking us either at Herat or elsewhere.

That is the position on the one side. It is virtually a permanent security for peace on condition of our making up our minds, now that the circumstances under which we adopted the principle of insular exclusiveness have changed, to change that principle of our policy.

On the other hand, if we will not do so, we run at least the almost infinite risk of having, by ourselves and with our own strength alone, to resist Russia, and very probably Russia and France, under circumstances most disadvantageous to ourselves. We shall not, as against Russia, be able to put forth anything like the same strength that we can put forth in support of other Powers, who can deliver against her far more effective blows than we can.

Meantime, whilst neither Austria nor Italy in the smallest degree disguise their wish that we should join their alliance, Germany, whilst she has, with perhaps the exception of Italy, more to gain by it than any other Power, shows clearly that she is anxious for it, whilst, as it has been well put to us, "she scoffs at it like a skilful purchaser in an Eastern bazaar."

The reason is clear. She knows that she has to deal with English statesmen who, whichever party may be in office, do not understand, or attempt to understand, the military bearings of the question. All her statesmen, understanding these perfectly, feel that they are in the position of a horse-dealer wanting to buy a horse from a man who knows nothing about the points of his own animal. We can, if we understand the advantages we have to offer, make what terms we please.

When we first saw the announcement of the anonymous articles which were appearing in the 'Fortnightly,' we hailed them with eager pleasure. They seemed to promise that at last some man well acquainted with many of the inner workings of foreign politics, and with the interior of our own Foreign Office, was attempting to master also the military problems involved in our foreign relations. Having for years attempted to urge that study upon such politicians as fate has thrown in his way, the present writer, as a soldier, certainly did not ask for the apology which Sir Charles Dilke has offered for making the attempt, nor does he know one soldier who has not welcomed the effort. When, however, he found that, under guise of patriotism, party spirit was rampant; when under the name of facts, fictions were put forward; when no one of the points so all-important to England as to the part she can now play in ensuring peace were noticed,— it seemed to him to be time to put forth a warning voice. If the Italian statesmen are wrong in thinking that a great naval alliance is what will best serve their turn; if Germany will not require to be protected at sea, for the reasons we have assigned; if the frontiers of Germany, of Russia, and of France are not such as we have shown them to be,—our errors can be easily exposed. If, on the other hand, what we have said is true, we think that a patriotic statesman should admit the truth of those points which have been omitted from his calculations. Our anxiety throughout has been to give such of our readers as have not seen Sir Charles Dilke's pages a fair account of what he has put forward, in order to show how far we agreed with him, and where we differed. In hardly any instances as yet has his method of reply to us consisted in anything else than in alleging that we had said that which we had not anywhere said, and in arguing against that which we do not believe.[1]

---

[1] The most audacious statement of this kind is the averment that the articles were written "in the name of the Adjutant-General of the Army" ('Fortnightly,' November 1887, p. 611). Our readers will have seen that there was not even a pretext for this assertion. A direct misquotation from a public speech of Lord Wolseley's had been made in inverted commas by Sir Charles Dilke. We challenged Sir Charles Dilke to show that the words he had quoted were to be found in any shorthand-writer's report of the speech. He was utterly unable to show that Lord Wolseley had ever used the words which he had repeatedly quoted. Under those circumstances we submit that, for a man who considers himself bound by the ordinary laws of civilised society in England, there is only one course open—viz., to withdraw and apologise for what, under the circumstances, was a very grave slander. In order, however, that by no subterfuge we might take advantage of Sir Charles Dilke's having made a rather careless quotation, which he could not substantiate, we, for that express purpose, inquired personally of Lord Wolseley to what matters he was referring when he spoke of our recent reforms as having been business-like and directed towards getting rid of the "theatrical" element. For that purpose, and that purpose only, throughout the entire series of articles, we quoted a private statement of Lord Wolseley's. The complete report of the nature of the reforms had not been made public, and we were therefore, for the purposes of this personal explanation, for which, under the circumstances, it was natural for any one to ask, obliged

That, no doubt, will be very convincing to those readers of the 'Fortnightly' who have not looked at our articles. It will, we fancy, produce a different effect upon those who read both.

to say that Lord Wolseley referred to quite other matters. What those were is now evident to every one who has read General Brackenbury's evidence.

The most comic case in which Sir Charles has thus dealt with our statements is one in which he has charged us with a ludicrous blunder which we did not commit, but which he did. He says, p. 620, November 1887 'Fortnightly,' that we had made a statement to the effect that we might rely upon the native States of India in the event of war with Russia, and make use of them against that Power,—an opinion in direct conflict with that of the Indian Commission, "who pointed out in their report that the friendship of an Indian prince is no defence against the hostility of his people." Sir Charles never gives references, so that none of his charges can be compared by an ordinary reader with the original. If we have been in any case unfair to him, the correction is easy, for we give the references. Now what we did in this matter—*ante*, p. 60—was to quote Sir Lepel Griffin on a point on which we venture to think his authority higher than that of most Indian soldiers. He had said that we might, in the event of war with Russia, rely upon the loyalty of the feudatory princes of India. We said nothing about the extent to which they could carry their people with them, or about the military value of their assistance ; but we said that the fact of their loyalty was an element of our strength "not to be ignored." We expressly reserved discussion, because we expect to have an opportunity of saying something about it elsewhere.

Now on pp. 171, 172 of 'The Present Position of European Politics,' there is an elaborate discussion of the effect of the *native army* and the "*sympathies of the oriental populations*" upon the chances of a contest between us and Russia. After setting forth the views of foreign writers as to the chance of these both being easily won by Russia, Sir Charles, as his leading argument against that opinion, says, "I believe in the superior popularity of England

In conclusion, we have this to say: Whether it be a partisan opinion or not, there are numbers of us, who never cared a rush for party before, who are looking to the present Government in the hope

among the *native princes* to any which may be thought to be enjoyed by Russia."

We certainly should not have ventured to use that argument in the way Sir Charles Dilke has done, because we have been long aware of the facts which he appears to have discovered between the publication of 'The Present Position of European Politics' and that of the article in the November number of the 'Fortnightly.' Nevertheless we continue to think, with Sir Lepel Griffin, that the loyalty of the native princes is an element "not to be ignored," though we neither allege that it carries with it the affection of the populations, nor a very great access of military power as the defence of India is at present constituted.

We cannot weary our readers with more specimens; but after these, and those to which the course of our argument has led us in the body of the text, we think that we may fairly ask that no statement of our words shall be accepted, without reference, on Sir Charles Dilke's authority. The curious in specimens of unfair quotation may compare Sir Charles's statement, November 'Fortnightly,' p. 612, as to our expressions about Lord Salisbury's and Lord Rosebery's policy, with *ante*, p. 10. It is needless to say that we in no wise denied the continuity of the two policies, but objected that a man who claimed independence of party should ignore the history of the previous years of foreign policy to which we alluded. Or they may compare his reference to the question of the 900 field-guns, p. 613, with our words, *ante*, pp. 41-48.

It would not, however, be fair to complain too much. Sir Charles has been trained by the habit of speaking in the heated meetings of partisans who, provided their opponents are roundly abused, are not nicely particular as to facts. The training of the present writer for such discussions has consisted chiefly in having to supply facts as accurate as possible, because on their accuracy the lives of men might depend. It is natural that we should approach controversy from different points.

that, taking all its elements into consideration, it is going to be thoroughly national in its policy. Nothing could have tended to inspire us with more hope in that respect than the business-like way in which Mr Smith was setting himself to work to secure untheatrical reality in matters of vital importance to the country. Nothing will more utterly shake our faith than any looking back by those who have set their hands to the plough. The Government have been going bravely forward in Ireland, and have gained strength in proportion to their courage, in the face of such encouragement to lawlessness as we have never seen before. They have inspired confidence by their firmness in London. But it is idle to deny that many of those who wish them best are afraid that both at the Admiralty and the War Office Lord Randolph's escapade has had too much influence. The Government perfectly well know how very much truth there is in the charges against our condition of preparedness which both Lord Randolph Churchill and Sir Charles Dilke have made. In a very short time indeed, if they do not carry out into practice the reforms which have been worked out on paper under Mr Smith's impulse, they will be responsible when the hour of reckoning comes, which is now fast approaching. We have cautiously throughout spoken, not of what our navy is, but of what it ought to be.

We have as cautiously spoken of the two *corps d'armée* and the cavalry division towards which we were working. The reduction of the Horse-Artillery will have been an inexcusable blunder if, in return for that great sacrifice, we are not to find, when the next Army Estimates are presented, that actual progress has been made towards a real and effective provision for the mobilisation of those forces. It is idle to deny that numbers of our best naval officers are alarmed by the announcement that no more ironclads are to be built. We have not written these articles for the sake of crying " Peace, peace," where there is no peace. We have endeavoured to show in what way most economically the terrible dangers which we must face can be met and dealt with. We do not believe in the policy of taking more upon our shoulders than we need take. Nevertheless, this much is certain, that if we do not help ourselves no other Power will help us. If we cannot and will not give help, we cannot get help. It is a question simply of securing for a moderate price the incalculable blessings of peace, or of being involved in certainly the most costly, and probably the most fatal, war in which we have ever been engaged.

INDEX.

A'Court, Captain, on the military resources of Italy, 194.
Adrianople, the Russian force beyond, 23.
Alsace-Lorraine, annexation of, 15.
"Amphibious strength, our," xxxiv.
Apponzi, Count, on the attitude of England, 218.
Armed force, the work of our, 4.
Armies, the field, of Europe, 163—Russian numbers v. Austrian, 164.
Armies, transport of, by sea, 34.
Army Act, alteration of the, 1.
Army-corps scheme, the eight, 49.
Artillery, field, and its use, xxx.
Artillery, volunteer, 42—Sir Edward Hamley on, 43—the field, 44—Russian do., 59—reduction of English horse, would be a blunder, 239.
Asia Minor, the danger of, 213—can Britain protect? 224.
Australian colonies, xxxiv.
Australian colonies, Russian designs on our, 53.
Austria in historic wars, 154—the races of, 158—her great soldiers, 159—her commanding position, 161.
Austrian defence, 166.
Austrian strength, 155—effect of recent changes on Austrian power, 156—recent, fortification, 160—forces, 162—inferiority of Austrian rifles to those of Russia, 165.
Austro-German frontier, the, 133.

Baikov, Colonel, on the Russian cavalry, 57.
"Balance of power," meaning of, as formerly used, 2—a fictitious, 5—when our pledge was broken, 11 et seq.
Balance of military power in Europe, the, 1 et seq.
Balkan States, the, 220.
Baltic fortresses, German, 139.
Beaconsfield's, Lord, Government, and the defence of coaling-stations, viii.
Belgian neutrality, 109 — Von Moltke's view of, in 1870, 114.
Belgium and England, 110—time v. violation of Belgium, 111—railway difficulty of violation, 113 —our relation to Belgium, 117—Mr Kinglake and Lord Salisbury on, 118—the latest pledge to, 119—duty of England towards, 229.
Beresford, Lord Charles, xxxii.
Berlin Congress, the, 11.
Bismarck's, Prince, sons, 79—his advocacy of an Italian alliance, 198 — Sir Charles Dilke's erroneous views regarding the opinions of, 208.
Blind, Karl, on Poland, 137.
Boulanger, General, and mobilisation, 105—his gaseous froth, 123.
Brackenbury, General, on the scheme of defence, 39 et seq.
Bridge, an economical, 46.
Bridge, the Russian, on the Vistula, 145.

Q

242   Index.

Bright, Mr, and the "balance of power," 126.
British army the cheapest in the world, xviii.
British war power, 33 — how to develop it, 34.
Bunsen, Herr von, on Mr Gladstone, 207.

Campaign of 1877-78, the military facts of, 222.
Camps, intrenched, 101.
Carpathians, the, a natural citadel to Austria, 161.
Cavalry, Russian, 58 — Austrian do., 165.
Cavalry, the proper use of, xxvi.
Channel Tunnel, the, xxviii.
China, conditions of an alliance with, 228.
Chinese Wall, the, 108.
Churchill, Lord Randolph, his Wolverhampton speech, 22 *et seq.*—on the state of our defences, 38—his deceptive comparison of the army budgets of Britain and Germany, 83.
Clive's economy, 70.
Coaling-stations, 206—and partisanship, 207.
Coaling-stations, foreign, 35.
Commerce, our strength and weakness, 61.
Comora Islands, the French occupation of the, 177.
Comparisons, true and false, 81.
Confidence, French and German, 125.
Constantinople, the Russian approach to, 221—British protection of, and Varna, 232.
Continental armies, the dimensions of the, 216.
Continental war, importance of the first days of a, 209.
Controversy, the necessities of, 236.
Cyprus, the occupation of, 11, 17.

Danish army, strength of the, 230.
Danish war, the story of the, 16.
Defence, the rival schemes of, 36.
Defences, grave deficiencies in the condition of our, 38.

Denmark, the attitude of, 230.
Diego Suarez, the French occupation of, 177.
Dilke, Sir Charles, on "the position of European politics," xi., 3 *et seq.*—his blunders, 235 *et seq.* — his misrepresentation of Lord Wolseley, 236 *note*.
Dragoons, the new Russian, 55—opinions on, 56.

Economy and efficiency, 69—costly economy, 91.
Education, questionable economy in, 89—recruits, non-commissioned officers, and, 90.
Efficiency, army, English and German, 92.
Egypt, the English force landed in, in 1882, 30.
Egyptian revolt, the, 30.
Elsass-Lothringen railways, 77.
Empire and commerce, 85.
England, the new power of, 192.
English power "cometh but by sea," 30, 216.
Europe, the war-map of, 8 —the field-armies of, 163.

"Facing-both-Ways," Mr, 215.
Fighting, means of, 94.
Fleet, a strong English, a necessity, 204.
Force, the work of our armed, 4— the reign of, in Europe, 10— British force depends on amphibious strength, 51.
Fortresses, home, 35—the forest of, 98—German and Baltic do., 139—Russian do., 149.
French army of to-day, 121—its strength, 124.
French defence scheme, the, 97— its weak point, 102.
Frontiers, French and German, 96 —German and Russian do., 133.

Geok Tépé, the defeat of, 181.
German and Baltic fortresses, 139.
German and English economy, 66.
German and Russian frontiers, the, 133—recent changes, 134—advantage of German frontier, 152.
German army of to-day, 121—do.

Index. 243

of 1870 and 1888, 122 — its strength, 124.
German defence scheme, the, 99—do. silent work, 106—the, opportunity, 107.
German empire, ring-fenced, 84.
German pension-list, 77.
"Germanic Confederation, overthrow of the," Sir A. Malet's, 14.
Germany, why, needs Austria, 153 — position of, in a war with Russia and France combined, 168—her power of transfer of force and of gaining time, 171—her power of keeping two "fretful realms" in awe, 173—the great and conservative power of, 185.
Germany, France, and Belgium, 65.
Germany, Russia, and Austria, 131.
Gladstone, Mr, his attitude on the Danish question, 15—Mr Bright on Mr Gladstone's many turnings of his coat, 16—his influence on Italy, 191.
Graham, Sir Lumley, 135.
Granville, Lord, on the Belgian question, 119.
Griffin, Sir Lepel, on the feudatory princes of India, 60.
Guns, big, and loose critics, 44.

Hagenau on the British strength in Egypt, 51.
Hamilton, Port, the surrender of, 176—its importance, 228.
Hamley, Sir Edward, on volunteer artillery, 43.
Harcourt, Sir William Vernon, on the "Jingoes," 18.
Hardy, Mr, on defence work, 50.
Hartington, Lord, on the danger in Asia Minor, 213.
Herat, how to protect, 179.
Heri Rud, the, xvii, 179.
Hong-Kong, xv.
Hooper's, Mr, history of the Sedan campaign referred to, 107.
Horsford's, Sir Alfred, scheme for landing English troops in Denmark, 15.
Hungarian approval of English policy, 212.
Hungary, patriotism in, 155.

Ignatieff's action towards Turkey, 220 *note*.
India, British disadvantage in, 53—our native army in, 85.
"Indian authorities," 178—do. on Europe, 183.
Indian frontier, Russian menaces on the, 53.
Infantry, the Russian, 54—Russian mounted do., 58.
Intrenched camps, true use of, 101.
Italian alliance, effect of an, on British foreign policy, 219.
Italian power, use of the, 197.
Italian statesmen and Turkey, 219.
Italy, its enormous seaboard, 192—its war resources, 194—alliance of, Germany, Austria, and England, 197—the probability of war with Russia and France as allies, 202—the naval service England could offer to, 205—German view of Italian politics, 208.
Italy, Turkey, and English alliances, 191.

Jena, Prussia before, 203.
"Jingo," the, 18—use of the word, 19—hopeless confusion of the term, 20—the author of, 126.

Kertch expedition, the, 31.
Kimberley, Lord, and the Danes, 11.
Kinglake, Mr, the lessons of the Kertch expedition, 31—on the Belgian question, 118.
Kirchhammer, Captain, on the Russo-German frontier, 135.
Knox's, Mr, knowledge of army schemes, 86.
Kropotkine, Prince, 219.

Luxembourg, the neutrality of, 113.

Malleson, Colonel, on Russian aggression in Asia, 52.
Malta, the Indian troops at, 23.
Marga, Captain, on Austrian defence, 166.
Maurice's, C. Edmund, revolutionary movement of 1848-49 in

Italy, Austria, Hungary, and Germany, referred to, 158.
Medical men, the payment of, in the army, xxiv.
Medical pension-list, xx.
Military power in Europe, balance of, 1 et seq.
"Military professors," press attacks on, xxvii.
Mobilisation, difficulties of English, 86—the present scheme, 87—German do. in 1888, 105.
Moltke on the Russian dragoons, 56—his position as head of the "great staff," 94.

Napoleon, Louis, on the causes of the French disasters, 102.
Newfoundland coast question, 211.
Nihilism in Russia, 213.
Novikoff, Madame, and her faithful henchman, 175.

Otway, Sir Arthur, and the balance of power controversy, 125.

Pay in Germany, officers', 74—do. in England, 75.
Peace or war, 240.
Pension-list, the German, 77.
Perrucretti, Colonel, on French power of transport of troops by sea, 196.
Poland, Karl Blind on, 137—Russian fortresses in, 144—Poland as a theatre of war, 150—the armies that would engage, 151.
Polish mud Napoleon's great enemy, 150 note.
Polish region, importance of, 138.
Position, author's own, 21.
Powers, strength of, 9—English power, 33—how to develop it, 34—navy, wires, harbours, mobility, 35.

'Quarterly Review' on Russia, 174 et seq.

Railways, Russian, 136.
Recruits, non-commissioned officers, and education, 90.
Reserve forces, the, 45.
Rhine, the command of the, 100.

Ricci, Lieutenant-General, on the natural strength of Italy, 193—on the Italian army, 195.
Roumanian army, the, 51.
Russell, Lord, on the defence of Belgium, 119.
Russia, the broken pledges of, 210.
Russia and England, 29.
Russia's wedge, 140—how met by Germany, 141—method for defence and offence, 143—when should we strike her real power, 181—her power of absorbing Eastern countries, 182.
Russian base, weakness of, 148.
Russian forces in 1878, 22—our power to stop them, 23—condition of the Russian army, 54—disbelief of the overwhelming forces which Russia is said to be able to employ against Germany and Austria, 231.
Russian frontier, the, 133.

Salaries, civil, 73.
Salisbury, Lord, on the foreign policy of Britain, 118.
Savoy, neutral, 227.
Schemes, the rival, and their authors, 36.
Seaboard States, the minor, 230.
Secrecy in State and camp, 175.
Sedan campaign, the, 107.
Services, cheap and dear, 71—money cost of universal, 80.
Shakespeare, General, 47.
Silesia, importance of, 146.
Singapore, xv.
Situation, danger of present, 212.
Smith's, Mr W. H., work as a military reformer, 39, 206.
Soldiers from a dear market, 82.
"Staff, the great general," 95.
Stanhope's, Mr, defence scheme, 49.
Stephen's, Sir James Fitz-James, Commission, 4 et seq.
Strength and weakness, our, 7.
Switzerland and the Vienna Congress, 226.
Switzerland, is, safe? 116.

Taxation, methods of, 78.
Telegraphic orders for the movement of troops, 210.

Thiers, M., his power in France after the fall of the Commune, 131—on the law of right, 214.
Thompson's, Sir Ralph, salary and services, 71.
Transport of armies by sea, 34.
Trevelyan, Sir Charles, his responsibility for the misery, the extravagance, and loss of life in the Crimean winter, xxxii.
Turkey and the Central Alliance, 221.
Turkish army, the condition of the, 223—its strength, 224.
Turkish Empire, the maintenance of the, 221.
Turkish war of 1877-78, the, 6.

United States expenditure, xix.
Universal service, money cost of, 80.
Upton, General (U.S.), on our native army in India, 85.

Vantage, our, in Europe, 52.
Verestchagin and Russia, 32.
Vienna, the treaty of, 226 *et seq.*
Vienna Congress, the, 226.
Vincent, Mr Howard, on the ultimate forces of the British Empire, 5.
Vistula, Russian bridges over the, 145—Russian advance by, 147.
Vladivostock, the importance of, 52, 59, 61.
Vosges, the difficulties of the, 171.

Wachs, Major, on the French frontier fortresses, 98.
War-map of Europe, the, 8.
War Office, practical work at the, viii.
Warsaw camp, the, 134.
Waste, causes of, 88.
Welby, Sir Reginald, xxxiii.
Wellington, Duke of, on preparation for war, 32.
Wolseley, Lord, his essay on the past and present of the English army, ix—and the use of artillery, 48—his opinion of Mr Smith's army reforms, 206—Sir Charles Dilke's misrepresentation of, 236 *note*.

THE END.

MILITARY BOOKS.

THE OPERATIONS OF WAR EXPLAINED AND ILLUSTRATED. By MAJOR-GENERAL SIR E. B. HAMLEY, K.C.M.G., late Commandant Staff College. Fourth Edition, Revised throughout. Small 4to, with numerous Maps and Plans. £1, 10s.

"A work of deep scientific research, which needs no commendation of ours to maintain the high place it has assumed in modern military literature."—*Saturday Review.*

"No English work has yet at all matched General Hamley's 'Art of War.'"—*Times.*

ON OUTPOSTS. By the SAME. Second Edition. 8vo, 2s.

A HANDY TEXT-BOOK ON MILITARY LAW. Compiled chiefly to assist Officers preparing for Examination; also for all Officers of the Regular and Auxiliary Forces. Specially arranged according to the Syllabus of Subjects of Examination for Promotion, Queen's Regulations, 1883. Comprising also a Synopsis of part of the Army Act. By MAJOR F. COCHRAN, Hampshire Regiment; Garrison Instructor, North British District. Crown 8vo, 7s. 6d.

"Mainly compiled with the view of assisting officers who are qualifying for promotion, this manual of military law is admirably adapted for that purpose, because the author has succeeded in presenting a clear and systematic exposition of all the subjects embraced in the military law examination. So complete, indeed, is the work, that reference to other books is unnecessary."—*Naval and Military Gazette.*

"Officers qualifying for promotion when preparing for the examination in military law will find this an invaluable text-book."—*Broad Arrow.*

THE ELEMENTS OF FIELD ARTILLERY. DESIGNED FOR THE USE OF INFANTRY AND CAVALRY OFFICERS. By HENRY KNOLLYS, Captain Royal Artillery. With Engravings. Crown 8vo, 7s. 6d.

"He has compiled carefully from the best authorities, and gives to his quotations the gloss and commentary of his own personal knowledge and experience. He has chosen a topic of daily occurring military interest, and the manner in which he has dealt with it fully justifies us in recommending his work as a valuable handy book of artillery knowledge."—*United Service Gazette.*

ESSAYS WRITTEN FOR THE WELLINGTON PRIZE, AND SELECTED FOR PUBLICATION BY HIS GRACE'S DESIRE FROM THOSE SPECIALLY MENTIONED BY THE ARBITER. Demy 8vo, 12s. 6d.

FIFTEEN YEARS OF ARMY REFORM. By an OFFICER. Demy 8vo, price 2s. 6d.

"A severe indictment of recent army administration."—*Saturday Review.*

"Powerfully written.......Every one who takes a real interest in the military power of England should study it attentively."—*Standard.*

WILLIAM BLACKWOOD & SONS, EDINBURGH AND LONDON.

SELECTED BOOKS.

THE COMPLETION OF MR KINGLAKE'S HISTORY.

THE INVASION OF THE CRIMEA: ITS ORIGIN, AND AN ACCOUNT OF ITS PROGRESS DOWN TO THE DEATH OF LORD RAGLAN. By A. W. KINGLAKE.

VOL. VII.—FROM THE MORROW OF INKERMAN TO THE FALL OF CANROBERT.

VOL. VIII.—FROM THE OPENING OF PÉLISSIER'S COMMAND TO THE DEATH OF LORD RAGLAN.

With an Index to the whole Work. Illustrated with numerous Maps and Plans. Demy 8vo, 28s.

CABINET EDITION.

THE INVASION OF THE CRIMEA. By A. W. KINGLAKE. 7 Vols. With Maps and Plans, crown 8vo, each 6s.

THE LAND BEYOND THE FOREST. FACTS, FIGURES, AND FANCIES FROM TRANSYLVANIA. By E. GERARD, Author of 'Reata,' 'Beggar my Neighbour,' &c. 2 Volumes 8vo, with Map and Illustrations, 25s.

A STORY OF ACTIVE SERVICE IN FOREIGN LANDS. COMPILED FROM LETTERS SENT HOME FROM SOUTH AFRICA, INDIA, AND CHINA, 1856-1882. By SURG.-GENERAL A. GRAHAM YOUNG, Author of 'Crimean Cracks.' Crown 8vo, Illustrated, 7s. 6d.

ENGLAND AND RUSSIA FACE TO FACE IN ASIA. A RECORD OF TRAVEL WITH THE AFGHAN BOUNDARY COMMISSION. By LIEUTENANT A. C. YATE, Bombay Staff Corps. With Maps and Illustrations. 8vo, 21s.

EPISODES IN A LIFE OF ADVENTURE; or, MOSS FROM A ROLLING STONE. By LAURENCE OLIPHANT, Author of 'Piccadilly,' 'Altiora Peto,' 'Haifa,' &c. Fourth Edition. Post 8vo, 6s.

INSULINDE. EXPERIENCES OF A NATURALIST'S WIFE IN THE EASTERN ARCHIPELAGO. By Mrs H. O. FORBES. Post 8vo, with a Map, 8s. 6d.

REMINISCENCES OF AN ATTACHÉ. By HUBERT E. H. JERNINGHAM, Author of 'Diane de Breteuille.' Second Edition. Crown 8vo, 5s.

THE LIFE AND WORK OF SYED AHMED KHAN, C.S.I. By LIEUT.-COLONEL G. F. I. GRAHAM, B.S.C. 8vo, 14s.

SPORT, TRAVEL, AND ADVENTURES IN NEWFOUNDLAND AND THE WEST INDIES. By CAPTAIN W. R. KENNEDY, R.N. With Illustrations by the Author. Post 8vo, 14s.

THE STORY OF MY LIFE. By the late Colonel MEADOWS TAYLOR, Author of 'The Confessions of a Thug,' &c., &c. Edited by his Daughter. Fourth and Cheaper Edition. Crown 8vo, 6s.

WILLIAM BLACKWOOD & SONS, EDINBURGH AND LONDON.

IN ONE VOLUME. THE LIBRARY EDITION OF

STORMONTH'S DICTIONARY

OF THE

ENGLISH LANGUAGE,

PRONOUNCING, ETYMOLOGICAL, AND EXPLANATORY.

Embracing Scientific and other Terms, numerous Familiar Terms, and a Copious Selection of Old English Words. To which are appended Lists of Scripture and other Proper Names, Abbreviations, and Foreign Words and Phrases.

BY THE REV. JAMES STORMONTH.

The PRONUNCIATION carefully revised by the Rev. P. H. PHELP, M.A. CANTAB.

Royal 8vo, handsomely bound in half-morocco, 31s. 6d.

Opinions of the British and American Press.

Times.—"This may serve in great measure the purposes of an English cyclopedia. It gives lucid and succinct definitions of the technical terms in science and art, in law and medicine. We have the explanation of words and phrases that puzzle most people, showing wonderfully comprehensive and out-of-the-way research. . . . We need only add, that the dictionary appears in all its departments to have been brought down to meet the latest demands of the day, and that it is admirably printed."

Pall Mall Gazette.—"The pronunciation of every word is given, the symbols employed for marking the sounds being commendably clear. . . . After the pronunciation comes the etymology. It has, we think, been well managed here. And the matter is, on the whole, as judiciously chosen as it is skilfully compressed and arranged."

Scotsman.—"There can be no question that the work when completed will form one of the best and most serviceable works of reference of its class. . . . It is admirably adapted to meet the requirements of every ordinary reader, and there are few occasions of special reference to which it will not be found adequate. The definitions are necessarily brief, but they are almost always clear and pointed. . . . A word of praise is due to the beauty and clearness of the printing."

STORMONTH'S DICTIONARY—*Continued.*

Opinions of the British and American Press—*Continued.*

Civil Service Gazette.—"We have had occasion to notice the peculiar features and merits of 'Stormonth's Dictionary,' and we need not repeat our commendations both of the judicious plan and the admirable execution. . . . This is a pre-eminently good, comprehensive, and authentic English lexicon, embracing not only all the words to be found in previous dictionaries, but all the modern words—scientific, new coined, and adopted from foreign languages, and now naturalised and legitimised."

Notes and Queries.—"The whole constitutes a work of high utility."

Dublin Irish Times.—"The book has the singular merit of being a dictionary of the highest order in every department and in every arrangement, without being cumbersome; whilst for ease of reference there is no dictionary we know of that equals it. . . . For the library table it is also, we must repeat, precisely the sort of volume required, and indispensable to every large reader or literary worker."

Liverpool Mercury.—"Every page bears the evidence of extensive scholarship and laborious research, nothing necessary to the elucidation of present-day language being omitted. . . . As a book of reference for terms in every department of English speech, this work must be accorded a high place—in fact, it is quite a library in itself. . . . It is a marvel of accuracy."

New York Tribune.—"The work exhibits all the freshness and best results of modern lexicographic scholarship, and is arranged with great care, so as to facilitate reference."

New York Mail and Express.—"Is the nearest approach to the ideal popular dictionary that has yet appeared in our language."

New York Sun.—"A well-planned and carefully-executed work, which has decided merits of its own, and for which there is a place not filled by any of its rivals."

Boston Journal.—"A critical and accurate dictionary, the embodiment of good scholarship, and the result of modern researches. . . . It holds an unrivalled place in bringing forth the result of modern philological criticism."

Boston Gazette.—"There can be but little doubt that, when completed, the work will be one of the most serviceable and most accurate that English lexicography has yet produced for general use."

Toronto Globe.—"In every respect this is one of the best works of the kind in the language."

WILLIAM BLACKWOOD & SONS, EDINBURGH AND LONDON.

www.ingramcontent.com/pod-product-compliance
Lightning Source LLC
Chambersburg PA
CBHW032111230426
43672CB00009B/1703